BOLD as a LAMB

For current information on the
Persecuted Church contact:

The Voice of the Martyrs, Inc.
PO Box 443
Bartlesville, OK 74005
(918) 337-8015

BOLD as a LAMB

Pastor Samuel Lamb
and the Underground
Church of China

KEN ANDERSON

ZondervanPublishingHouse
Grand Rapids, Michigan

A Division of HarperCollinsPublishers

Bold As A Lamb
Copyright © 1991 by Ken Anderson

Requests for information should be addressed to:
Zondervan Publishing House
Grand Rapids, Michigan 49530

Library of Congress Cataloging-in-Publication Data

Anderson, Ken, 1917–
   Bold as a lamb : Pastor Samuel Lamb and the underground church of
China / Ken Anderson.
       p.   cm.
   ISBN 0-310-53221-3 (pbk.)
   1. Lamb, Samuel, 1924– . 2. Clergy—China—Canton—Biography.
3. 35 Da Ma Zhan (Church : Canton, China) 4. Persecution—China—
Canton. 5. Canton (China) 6. Communism and
Christianity—China. I. Title.
BR1297.L35A53   1991
272*c39.'092—dc20
                                                                    90–45648
   [B]   CIP

Edited by Linda Vanderzalm
Designed by Louise Bauer

Printed in the United States of America

94 95 96 97 98 / EP / 10 9 8 7 6 5 4

To my family, all of whom share with me a concern for China and a deep love for Samuel Lamb

1

Aн Leng stepped off the bus at Zhong Shan 5 and hesitated. A line of trucks and taxis passed. In Guangzhou, as in all of China's cities, drivers of motor vehicles paid almost no attention to pedestrians.

"Da Ma Zhan is a very narrow street," Wu San, his friend in the chemistry laboratory at the university had told him, "not wide enough for automobiles. You will enter through a small gate."

Ah Leng saw the gate and ventured cautiously onto the street as another string of taxis approached. A bus appeared, but halted for passengers. Bicyclers rang their caution bells. A taxi changed lanes, looming at him. Ah Leng darted aside, stiff-arming a bicycle to avoid being brushed. The rider, forced off balance, scolded him.

Ah Leng reached the gate of which Wu San had spoken and looked through to Da Ma Zhan. The street appeared to be as old as the Manchus.

Since his boyhood, Ah Leng had been fond of old and

narrow streets. He moved forward beneath protruding poles of laundry rustling in the evening breeze. Families sat at their doorsides, grandfathers looking blankly out onto the way and into the past, mothers sifting rice, and dogs drowsing.

A clutter of men, some playing, some observing, surrounded a noisy game of mah-jongg, similar at first glance to dominoes but more complicated. Tiny shops offered clothing, tobacco, and sundries. The blended aroma of pork, fish, steamed rice, and vegetables wafted from hawker stands. Ah Leng moved along, ignoring the sounds and smells, his eyes intent on the house numbers—63, 49, . . .

"Take care not to miss it," Wu San had cautioned. "The entrance is hard to find, so watch closely for the number 35 Da Ma Zhan."

Ah Leng slowed his pace, and there it was: residence unit 35. Even if he had missed the small number, Ah Leng would have found the house, because from the floor above street level and the floor above that, he heard the melody of many voices.

> To suffer is to serve our Lord.
> Our tears, like His, touch Heaven.
> We are the children of His Word
> To whom all grace is given.

The lyrics and the music stirred in the student a strange feeling. Confucius had once said, "Poetry arouses, music is our crown." What might the venerated one have said if he had heard the singing of these Christians? How strange for Ah Leng to think such thoughts—Ah Leng, a student of the late 1980s—a scientist, materialist, and atheist.

He moved to the bleak, narrow stairway, hesitating as his eyes adjusted to the darkness. A small dim neon light at the top of the stairway gave scant but sufficient illumination to silhouette nearly a dozen people sitting on the concrete steps.

"Church," Ah Leng said to them. "My friend says I go up these stairs to a church."

"One does. Welcome," a woman near the bottom

responded. "The Lord be with you this beautiful evening of his making." She gestured for him to sit on the step immediately below her feet. Since this was Ah Leng's first time to visit 35 Da Ma Zhan, he did not realize that these people, like himself, had arrived late. "Welcome," the woman repeated.

"Sit with us here," a man near the top called out. "Seats above are already full."

"But young people can always make room for one more," the woman said pleasantly. She pressed her feet tightly against the hallway wall and motioned for Ah Leng to proceed upward. He squeezed by the others in the passageway and slowly moved up the stairs.

When the singing stopped, Ah Leng heard a man's voice coming from the overhead speakers. It was a strong voice, authoritative but kind. "We welcome you in the name of our Lord Jesus. If you are with us for the first time, we give you double welcome! You will find our only purpose is to declare the Gospel and to learn together how to live the Christian life."

Pressing tightly against the stairway wall, Ah Leng reached the top and came into a narrow corridor packed tightly with more people—some on a narrow bench, most on stools the size of bicycle seats. An elegant woman dressed in peasant trousers and a plain mandarin jacket looked up at him and smiled. For a moment he wondered if he had seen her among the faculty at a campus convocation. Next to her a man, most likely her husband, studied some mimeographed notes so intently that he didn't notice Ah Leng.

A college-aged girl stepped out from an adjoining doorway. Her appearance drew Ah Leng's attention to her and to a small room where over a hundred people crowded into a space meant for fifty people. The girl was attractive, with curious, wise eyes. She wore student clothing and had a braided pigtail hanging to the middle of her back. She smiled warmly as if they had met before, although they had not.

"You visit us for the first time," she whispered, not as a question but as a greeting. "We have closed-circuit video at this lower level, as you can see, but perhaps you wish to go upstairs. Many students have come again tonight." She smiled, her eyes twinkling. "They always seem able to squeeze in one more."

Ah Leng watched the video screen where the man spoke. "For our next song of praise to the Lord, turn to number 63 in the *Spiritual Voice* hymnal."

"This way," the girl motioned, having inched her own way to the foot of a second stairway.

> *Praise Him! Praise Him!*
> *Jesus our blessed Redeemer!*

The people around Ah Leng began to sing, maintaining close tempo with those on the floor above. The experience was new to him, although it did not surprise him. He had heard that Christianity was a religion whose teachings were conveyed in various ways. Also, before he had given himself so fully to academic pursuit, he had learned to play the bass viol and the non-Oriental music scale.

The rendition itself was not so striking. In fact, the singing was quite dissonant.

> *Sing, O Earth,*
> *His wonderful love proclaim!*

No, it was the lyrics, sung as if they flowed from the very soul of the people.

Someone tapped Ah Leng's arm and pointed toward the girl at the foot of the stairs. He touched his mouth in momentary loss of face. He had for the moment forgotten her. He proceeded toward her, careful to avoid stepping on any feet.

He glanced into a small room that lay adjacent to the bottom of the second stairway. People sat as if they had been packed in by a machine. The room had outer panels, which he later learned were put back into place after each gathering to provide privacy for the pastor's night rest. The room was stark, like the storage area for a small shop. A refrigerator that stood in the right corner was pushed back to facilitate viewing of the video screen. A plain iron cot, the pastor's bed, provided seating for five women and a child. The child held a copy of *Spiritual Voice*, wrong side up, but pretended to sing as reverently as the others.

> *Crown Him! Crown Him!*
> *Prophet and Priest and King!*

Ah Leng found the second stairway more crowded than the first. "Try not to step on too many people," the girl chided. She gave him a copy of the sermon notes, then moved away to help other late arrivals.

> *Like a Shepherd,*
> *Jesus will guard His children.*

As Ah Leng climbed the second stairway, he glanced back and up, seeing what appeared to be a storage room above the pastor's meager quarters. It now functioned as a balcony accommodating nearly thirty people.

A young family dressed in clothing characteristic of the business community sat in the front of this balcony as comfortably as if occupying a concert-hall box seat.

> *Praise Him! Praise Him!*
> *Tell of His excellent greatness!*
> *Praise Him! Praise Him!*
> *Ever in joyful song!*

Ah Leng sensed the clutch of destiny on his heart. More than merely curious, he felt strangely pleased to have come. When he reached the top of the stairs, he saw the *muk si*, the pastor of whom Wu San had spoken so enthusiastically. The pastor sang out above the others, his voice enhanced by the microphone at the podium.

Although the pastor was less than five-and-a-half-feet tall and very thin, Ah Leng was attracted by the man's warm and resonant voice, his air of benign authority. He reminded Ah Leng of one of his favorite professors, a man who taught social philosophy at the university.

"Let's repeat the stanza," the pastor said. "Who of us does not have many reasons for praising the Lord?"

Ah Leng saw heads nodding in affirmation. Several

people around him softly echoed "Amen." Ah Leng noticed that the accompaniment for the singing came not from a piano, as he had at first thought, but from a large cassette player. The crowded room could not have accommodated a piano even if it had been suspended from the ceiling.

Another usher, also a young woman, caught his attention. She persuaded a bench of young people to squeeze closer together. As they did, Ah Leng noticed that each bench had an aisle-side supplement that could slide out to accommodate one more person. The aisle was thereby blocked, merging left side and right side into one continuous flow of people.

After he had sat down, he glanced at the mimeographed notes. *The God Who Lives* was the subject of the evening lecture. What a strange topic in a nation committed to atheism and to a god who exists only in test tubes and observable formulae! Were this many people interested in such a topic?

The God Who Lives! A chill touched Ah Leng's spine. When Wu San had spoken to him about God in their few conversations on campus, Ah Leng had not seriously considered the reality of such a deity. But in the midst of all of these joyful people, Ah Leng began to think that perhaps Wu San's God was real.

Ah Leng glanced through the eight half-pages of notes, folded like a small brochure:

1. Internal Doubt Should Not Look for External Evidences.
2. God Becomes Real When Faith Becomes Real.
3. Life's Surest Realities Belong Exclusively to God's Children.
4. Faith in a True and Living God Is the Right of Every Human Being.

He was eager for the *muk si* to begin his address.

People sat across the full front of the small platform, leaving only enough room for the speaker to stand. His podium rested on a base down among the audience.

Ah Leng had seen church buildings before, but he doubted that any of them had an interior like this one. "You call this a church building?" he whispered to the young man beside him.

"A house church," the young man replied. "I have heard it spoken of as the largest house church in China. It is surely the best known. This building has been Pastor Lamb's residence for many years. Pastor Lamb would never speak of largeness or prominence," the young man added. "He is a humble man, and many people respect him for that."

The pastor stepped to the microphone. "Now we shall pray," he said, closing his eyes. Many people also closed their eyes and bowed their heads. Ah Leng continued to look around.

"Our God, we praise you!" the *muk si* began.

"Amen," whispered the young man.

"You are praying also?" Ah Leng asked.

The young man, seeming disturbed, looked up.

"Oh," Ah Leng added, now whispering, "I'm sorry."

"We talk to God together." The young man bowed once more, secluding himself behind his closed eyelids.

After the pastor finished his prayer, he began to preach. "We indeed have a living God. His living Word is forever changeless and forever true."

Ah Leng remembered from a freshman literature class, Rudyard Kipling's lines:

> *Heathen idol made of mud,*
> *That they call the great god Bud . . .*

But that night Ah Leng's mind was open to options. He had never experienced anything like this before. He knew people who went to temples, but they never expressed the kind of joy he saw in the rooms at Da Ma Zhan. He had heard priests before, but none expressed his beliefs with the kind of authority that this *muk si* exuded.

"The Bible tells us 'All have sinned and fall short of the glory of God,'" the pastor continued.* "You can't be rid of

---

*If you would like to know the references for the Scripture verses quoted in this book, you will find them listed at the end of the book.

doubt until you are rid of sin. You can't find faith until you find righteousness."

Ah Leng contrasted these words with those one of his professors had used: "Mankind's notions of religion are dead and must be buried. We must dispose of a corpse, no matter how sentimental our feelings may have been toward the illusion we think of as life."

Ah Leng thought back to his childhood, when in the secrecy of their home his mother had taught him to place incense in front of a photograph of his deceased father. He remembered the hurt he had caused his mother when he had come home from elementary school one day and told her that the teacher had mocked him in front of the class for admitting to such superstition. The teacher had angrily told him to rid his mind of religion.

"It is one thing to experience natural doubt," the pastor continued. "God honors honest inquiry. 'Test everything,' the Bible warns us. 'Hold on to the good.' If you have that kind of doubt, there is hope for you. But young people whose minds are *programmed* to doubt come to us. For over twenty years in prison, I experienced much of that kind of input. But God stood guard over my mind. Not once did my faith waver! Not so much as once!"

Twenty years in prison? Wu San had said nothing of this.

Ah Leng became suspicious. Were these words an introduction to anti-government teaching? And were these people subversives, camouflaged by the veneer of religion? Had Wu San tricked him into coming to 35 Da Ma Zhan?

Ah Leng's older sister once had been in the Red Guard, which resulted in much distress and disillusionment for her. None of that for him. Never.

But the pastor went on. "When our sovereign Creator designed us, he left us—in the words of one French philosopher—with a God-shaped vacuum inside."

Ah Leng turned to touch the arm of the young man beside him, but he refrained.

"Hebrews 11 tells us that 'faith is being sure of what we hope for and certain of what we do not see.' Truth disbelieved does not denote error. Faith rejected does not validate doubt. In his Word, God gives us specific procedures for rising out of the pit of doubt onto the certain sure ground of living faith. We find the key in Romans 10:7."

Throughout the audience, people turned the pages of their Bibles. Ah Leng had never held a Bible, and the book of Romans meant nothing to him.

"Let us read it together," said the pastor.

Half aloud, Ah Leng spoke to the young man next to him: "Are you a Christian?"

"For three months now," the young man replied. "Do you wish to become one?"

"I'm not sure."

"There will be discussion groups at the end of the meeting. Such a group assisted me. I could help you if you wish me to."

Ah Leng sat silently for several minutes. The sermon continued, but as he contemplated the young man's offer, he did not hear it.

"It is only as you wish," the young man said.

So it was that Ah Leng, the student, the disillusioned and inquiring one, became numbered with that ever-growing throng of China's young people who came to havens such as 35 Da Ma Zhan and found the meaning and light that had so long evaded them.

2

SAMUEL LAMB LAYS no claim to being a living martyr.

Across China, he and Watchman Nee and Wong Mingdao have become twentieth century symbols of commitment at whatever the price. In any case, China is a land with multitudes of Christian heroes. The combined years of their imprisonment would strike awe into the hearts of the most nonchalant church folk.

"We have all suffered much," says one layman, "and survived only by God's grace. There continues to be persecution in these days, and no one can predict the future, but it is now summertime compared to the winter we once endured. Our concern now is to apply what we have learned, to be obedient always to our wonderful Lord, to serve Him truly and faithfully."

"Perhaps we are fortunate," says another. "We suffered so much and have so little that Christianity is the most attractive option we see in life. If we were secure and well supplied, as we hear of Christians in other places, we might be much less sincere in our discipleship."

"You must remember something," says one elderly Christian, who languished more than ten years in a labor camp.

"Christian faith is most precious when we experience it under testing. The primary purpose of prayer is not for gaining wealth or comfort and earthly security. Faith and prayer are to make us true followers of our Lord who suffered as the greatest example of purpose in life. I have known many dark days, but I have also experienced how bright God's light can be in times of uncertainty and fear. I am sure the Lord is much more precious to me because of my experiences. Who could ask for more?"

Although Samuel Lamb did not hide his past, many people who came to 35 Da Ma Zhan in the 1980s—several of them young people like Ah Leng—knew little if anything about the pastor's past. They were drawn to the services by their own need and the witness of others.

People who continued to come would inevitably learn of Pastor Lamb's past experiences because he drew sermon illustrations from the whole span of his Christian life. However, only those people who were closest to him would realize that during many sermons or teaching sessions, his heart was heavy because he knew that at any moment the police could once again summon him to an interrogation.

He had been through it several times. Many times this modern Daniel had been summoned to appear at 7:00 A.M. at the police station, where an officer had directed him into an interrogation room with the demeaning manner one would display to a boy who had misbehaved at school.

Many times Samuel had seen the room with its drab walls, stark and empty except for a few notices. Behind a desk cluttered with paper sat a police officer.

"Good morning," he said somewhat pleasantly.

"Good morning, sir," Samuel responded.

A lackey appeared with a tray on which he brought a pot of steaming tea and two cups, basic tokens of Chinese hospitality. He poured one cup and handed it to the officer at the desk. He glanced toward Samuel.

The officer brusquely dismissed the servant, who looked back to make momentary eye contact with the renowned pastor. Had the servant perhaps been to 35 Da Ma Zhan?

The officer continued his pleasant manner, which Samuel

had learned to assess as an overlord's veneer. "What is your name?" he asked.

Samuel sighed. He had been asked this same question by this same man in this same place so many times before. "Lam Hin Go," Samuel said.

"You also have another name?"

"Lin Xiangao. It is in your records."

The officer picked up a file and opened it. "Ah yes, here." He thumbed through the file. "You are a man of many names."

"As you yourself well know, names vary according to the dialects."

"Yes, yes. Very true."

Anticipating the next statement, the pastor said, "You will remember, as you have noted in the past, that my closest associates call me Samuel Lamb."

Continuing to examine the file before him, the officer mused, "Ah yes, to be sure. Samuel Lamb." He looked up. Any pleasantry on his face, however contrived, vanished. His harsh, fiery eyes glared at Samuel. "Only imperialists use such a name as Samuel Lamb! What is it? European? American?"

"As I have told you before—"

"Answer me!" the officer interrupted.

"Samuel Lamb is my Christian name."

"Christian name, is it?"

"Members of God's family in many parts of the world might also select such a name."

"It is a name dishonoring to China."

Samuel offered no comment.

"You were born an imperialist, not a native Chinese."

This, too, Samuel had heard repeatedly in earlier encounters, but he calmly answered, "As you have previously entered in my record, I was born in Macau on October 4, 1924. My parents were Christians, and both were Chinese citizens. My maternal grandfather had been a pharmacist in Zhao Qing. He—"

"Your father and your paternal grandfather emigrated to America. Your grandfather supported the low reputation of our people in imperialist countries by opening a laundry in Detroit."

"My father returned against his own father's wishes. He enrolled in seminary to prepare himself for Christian ministry. He was a Baptist pastor in Macau when I was born." It was all in the file on the officer's desk, and had all been reiterated before.

"You were trapped in China when the Japanese invaded, or you yourself would be a rich laundryman in America. Is that not the truth?" The officer punctuated his statement with a dry chuckle.

"I told you at our last meeting," Samuel responded, "and at several before that one. I was invited to teach at a school in Hong Kong, but I chose to remain in China."

"To carry out imperialistic assignments?" the officer snapped back.

"Not for such a purpose, sir."

"Come now," the officer said as he lit a cigarette from the glowing butt of the one he had just finished. "China was flooded with an army of imperialists. Missionaries they were called. Isn't that correct? Missionaries who were in reality the agents of their governments—America, England, Germany. The whole world thirsts for the blood of our people. You and your family were agents of their purposes!"

While Samuel was interrogated, a small group of friends had come to join staff members at 35 Da Ma Zhan. "Give Pastor Lamb boldness," prayed one.

"Help him see he is not the one on trial," prayed another. "It is the Lord Jesus who is on trial, just as he once was in Pilate's hall."

"Amen," the kneeling believers quietly agreed.

It was not only the assembled Christians who prayed. At his work in a noodle factory, a man looked up from his machine and silently interceded. A mother nursing her newborn, glanced at a Bible she had just laid aside, and claimed its promises for her pastor. In one of the better apartment complexes along Haiphong Street, a housewife drew a chair from the eating table and knelt as she had done at the church's prayer time the previous night. "Pastor Lamb has told us," she prayed aloud, "that you put down Satan forever when Jesus died on the cross."

The group huddled at the church began to sing.

To suffer is to serve our Lord.
Our tears, like His, touch heaven.
We are the children of His Word,
To whom all grace is given.

Samuel Lamb was aware of this undergirding. His pulse beat normally. His hand remained steady. His confidence in the Lord anchored his spirit.

"Why do you continue to disobey your government?" persisted the interrogator. "During those twenty years, when our revolutionary teachers tried so faithfully to correct your thinking, you seem to have learned nothing of the value of obedience."

"Not once did I disobey those in authority over me," Samuel affirmed. He hesitated a moment and added, "And not once did I disobey my Lord!"

The interrogator stood, bringing himself eyeball-to-eyeball with the pastor. "The Chinese revolutionary government does not ask you to relinquish your obedience to God!" He winced at his own use of the word *God.* "We only ask you to join the Three-Self organization and become one with the patriotic churches now thriving all across this land."

"There are many good pastors in Three-Self," Pastor Lamb responded. He also had made this statement before. "But I have, to my regret, found Three-Self leaders whose theology denies the accuracy of the Bible and the full and unlimited deity of my Lord. As a conscientious pastor, I must be no part of this."

"You Christians are a weak lot," the policeman scoffed. "You fight like children. You want your own toys. The glorious revolution put away these needless segments. What were they called? Baptist, Methodist, Lutheran, Presbyterian. Those distinctions are all gone now, united in the Three-Self church, which you spurn."

Samuel did not respond. He had no desire to be belligerent. He wished to see unity among believers.

"Your illegal church has been closed before," the officer threatened, "and you may force us to close it again."

"The church is not our humble building," Pastor Lamb responded. "That is only the place where members of the true church meet together for fellowship and worship. When we were closed before, our believers met in their homes and interested people continued to come to Jesus."

The officer studied the file another moment. Then he closed it and left the room. Pastor Lamb waited a while, then also left, returning to 35 Da Ma Zhan in time to conclude the group's intercession with his own prayer of gratitude.

3

As a UNIQUELY FULFILLED PERSON, abounding in sanguine attitudes and sustaining assessments, Samuel Lamb demonstrates persuasive evidence that humanity's Creator programmed the Christian life to thrive under the most adverse circumstances.

To validate the rapport he believes a Christian may anticipate with God, he often quotes Isaiah 49:1: Listen to me, you islands, Hear this you distant nations. Before I was born, the Lord called me from my birth. He has made mention of my name.

"A Christian who has not suffered," he says, "is a child without training. Such Christians cannot receive or understand the fullness of God's blessing. They know the Lord only as an acquaintance rather than as an intimate heavenly Father!"

To be sure, the average Christian will not necessarily suffer physical oppression. If a child of God affirms the desire to live a life of commitment in contrast to seeking earth's pleasures and treasures, however, Samuel believes that such a Christian will experience the meaning of the Scripture verse that states: We share in His sufferings in order that we may also share in His glory (Rom 8:17).

From the moment of his birth in 1924, Samuel Lamb was marked for divine service. His family's surname was Lam, and at birth, the new son became Lin Xiangao; *Xian* means "to offer to," and *gao* means "the Lamb of God." An alternate pronunciation is *Lam Hin Go*. In 1938, the father, Paul Lam, also gave his son the name Samuel. With his birth name and his Christian name, Samuel was double lambs.

Samuel's parents were godly people who provided him with a stable and happy home, even though his father earned only a meager income as a pastor of a small Baptist church in a mountainous community overlooking Macau. His parents were living examples of trust and obedience. At an early age, before he understood the theology of salvation, Samuel determined to follow their example. Unlike most young boys, who pretended to be airplane pilots or soldiers of fortune, Samuel often pretended to be a preacher like his father.

Samuel was a wisp of a child, both short and thin. He was susceptible to respiratory infections, which he developed as a result of the altitude, prevailing winds off the South China Sea, and subtropical weather patterns in Macau. When he was only five, he became sick with what seemed to be a common cold. But the condition did not respond to his mother's remedies and worsened until the boy breathed as if he were being slowly strangled.

"We have done the best we know with medicine," Paul Lam said to his wife. "Now we must commit our son to the Great Physician." The godly man offered a simple, direct prayer. Both he and his wife fully expected the boy to recover soon.

"He has been given to the Lord," the mother affirmed in a way that Old Testament Hannah might have spoken. "The Lord can't allow him to die."

However, the boy did not recover. He grew alarmingly worse, and the father dispatched a message to a Christian doctor in Macau. After the doctor had spent only a few minutes with the sick child, he announced, "I'm afraid your son has diphtheria. You should have taken him to the hospital instead of calling for me."

The stunned family boarded a hired truck and began the journey down the mountain to the Baptist hospital in Macau. Moments of fear stalked each mile, haunting the parents with the thought that their son might not survive the trip.

"Our tests confirm diphtheria," the doctor told the parents at the hospital. "His condition is extremely critical."

"Will he live?" asked the father.

"I give him a five percent chance, ten at most."

"Can anything be done, doctor?"

"A tracheotomy perhaps. But even with that . . . As your doctor and as your Christian brother, I must tell you that your son has almost no chance of survival." The mother began softly sobbing.

"If our son must die," Paul Lam asked his wife, "would he be better off at home, where he has been so loved and so happy?" The mother nodded agreement. The doctor reluctantly agreed.

They took Samuel back up the mountain to their home, where neighbors and members of the congregation had gathered to await word. "Are you sure he must die?" one of the church elders asked. "We dare not let it be for lack of faith on our part."

The call went out for others to come and pray. Fathers left their work. Mothers bundled their children and hurried to the pastor's home. Old saints who had seen God's power through many years hobbled up steep mountain paths to join the intercessors.

Through the night and into the dawn these Christians prayed. At daybreak in the city below, the concerned doctor—having slept fitfully at best—began to make his way up the mountain. He would give spiritual comfort to those whose physical needs he had been unable to meet.

"Thank you for coming, Doctor!" the father exclaimed. "Is he . . . ?"

"See with your own eyes what the Lord has done."

When the doctor entered the bedroom, he saw Samuel eating breakfast.

"It's a miracle!" the doctor cried out. "Praise God!"

Young though he was at the time, Samuel understood

enough of what had happened to realize God had indeed touched his life.

"God touched you because he needs you," his mother said. Paraphrasing part of Isaiah 49, she told him, "Before you were born, the Lord called you; from your birth he has mentioned your name." Consequently, Samuel Lamb became even more convinced that he must serve God as effectively and faithfully as his parents did.

The family moved to Guangzhou—then known as Canton—and Samuel enrolled at a boarding school. The mainland stay was short. His father received a call from a church on Hong Kong's Cheung Chou island. Samuel remained to finish primary school.

The family had previously spent holidays at Cheung Chou, so the boy already had a treasury of pleasant memories about the island—ships passing, waterside hikes with his sisters, resident boys joining him for adventures in the island's abundant open spaces.

During the years Samuel remained as a boarding student in Canton, he returned to his parents and sisters during school vacations. He had numerous Chinese friends, and because Hong Kong was an active British colony in those days, Samuel also learned to speak English as naturally as if it were his native language.

The year Samuel finished primary school, he got his first taste of the sufferings war imposes on innocent people. Like any boy his age, he delighted at the spectacle of overhead aircraft. Delight turned to horror, however, the morning Japanese zeroes snarled out from the horizon to drop bombs over Canton. South China had endured mandarin struggles for centuries and had bled profusely from the opium wars, but this was totally different.

The boy managed his way to the presumed safety of Hong Kong. Then, as Japanese troops moved across South China in the wake of those devastating air attacks, return to Canton became impossible.

In Cheung Chou, Samuel entered a school where he majored in English instead of classical Chinese. After three years he transferred to Queen's College on Hong Kong island. Living on luxurious Hong Kong island whetted Samuel's fleshly appetites. Here he took long walks along the famous Peak Trail, looking down on one of the world's most spectacular vistas—Hong Kong city and fabulous Kowloon. He watched the Star Ferry plod from wharf to wharf between Kowloon and Hong Kong island, back and forth at three-minute intervals. Ships and freighters unfurling many flags festooned the bay. Gigantic ocean liners moored at the trinket-laden Ocean Terminal so passengers could dart ashore among the shops, like children searching after wonders for "show and tell" at home. Although at this point in his life Samuel would testify to being surrendered to the Lord, he was only partially surrendered, not realizing the strong hold that the wealthy life had on him.

Other times he would go down to the business district and walk among the towering commercial buildings. When he had an extra ten cents—ample those days for round trip passage—he rode the Star Ferry across to the other side. And on special occasions, he hailed a rickshaw for a ride through the Tsim Sha Tsui district.

Samuel did well in school, his command of English putting him on a par with schoolboys from British families. Sometimes he wondered what prevented him from becoming part of this affluent world, perhaps even becoming one of the Hong Kong tycoons whom he saw in their sleek limousines or private rickshaws.

At Queen's College, Samuel made new friends, some of them Christians. Most of his friends came from prosperous families and were being prepared for success in business. They introduced him to the theater and offered him cigarettes and alcohol, both of which he refused, struggling to maintain the staunch separationism of his Baptist upbringing. While he spurned the world, he nonetheless thirsted for it and looked on the secular life as an option for his future.

In a moment of whimsy he began giving haircuts—first to a few of his close friends, who had initial misgivings about his ability. Although he had never been trained to cut hair, Samuel's ability to style hair improved, and many school friends sought his services. The hair-cutting experience gave

Samuel not only a pleasant diversion but also a way of sharpening his campus image. He hadn't the slightest awareness that a sovereign Shepherd had him giving hair cuts as preparation for the future.

During this time Paul Lam accepted a professorship at a Bible institute in Singapore, believing it to be God's choice for this period of his life and knowing it would better support his family. As frequently happens in Chinese culture, the mother was left behind to care for the home and family.

Samuel's father wrote to him regularly, urging him to enroll in one of Hong Kong's Bible schools. He advised his son that in wealthy Hong Kong he would see firsthand how shallow life becomes for those who seek wealth and convenience above Christian commitment and service. Although Samuel heard his father's words, he was confident that he could succeed in the material world and also fulfill his role in the Lord's vineyard. He was too young to realize that the person who tries to bargain with God always comes out on the short end.

In his father's absence, Samuel's mother became the strongest influence in his life. He spent every weekend with his family, growing closer to his sisters, Ai Ling and Ai Jun. They attended Sunday worship together, and on Sunday evenings their mother gathered them together to sing hymns.

Samuel's mother was both parent and friend, as adept at counsel and encouragement as she was in surveillance and discipline. She detected the coldness that had come to Samuel's Christian experience. However, she never scolded, never preached, and never lectured. Instead, she prayed for him, believing that God had large plans for his life. She was confident of that since the time she nursed him as a newborn.

On one occasion when Samuel returned to school, he stood at the ferry's stem and watched the prow slice a watery path for the craft. He recognized that this was a picture of his life: The world beckoned to him and his flesh was weak, but

God had set a course for his life, and he must not waver from it.

Then came December 7, 1941, and the bombing of Pearl Harbor. Samuel had spent the weekend with his mother and sisters and was on the ferry returning to Hong Kong. Suddenly the captain cut the engine. At first, passengers thought the ferry's engine had failed, but soon they heard the heavy thud of bombs falling on Hong Kong's Kai Tak airport and other targets on the Kowloon side of Hong Kong. The ferry captain had to make a decision. Should he return to the presumed security of Cheung Chou or proceed on to Hong Kong? Passengers on board persuaded the captain to proceed to Hong Kong. Fear pervaded Samuel's thoughts as he looked back toward his home.

Within days, Japanese troops stormed the beach at Repulse Bay and inched their way across Hong Kong, killing many people as they moved. Air raids continued, striking at areas held by the outnumbered British and their Chinese counterparts.

With the ferry service stopped by the fighting, Samuel was trapped in Hong Kong. Weekends and evenings, when his heart ached to be with his mother and sisters, Samuel devoted many hours to Bible study and prayer. His faith grew. He had, indeed, come to his own Bethel and erected an altar of renewal in his heart. As he returned to God's Word and prayer, he grew confident.

One morning when Japanese bombers targeted an area adjacent to the school Samuel attended, the alarm sounded and students scurried for shelter. Samuel remained in the study hall. He stood at the window and watched the awesome performance. He didn't mean to be foolhardy. It was just that he had complete confidence in God's sovereignty over his life, and knew already that the most dangerous place on earth is safe if one is in God's will—and the safest place on earth is dangerous if one is out of his will.

On another occasion the bombing was so intense that Samuel decided to seek shelter in the Baptist church where he regularly worshiped. Ordinarily Samuel would have taken the route he used every Sunday morning—a route that avoided as many hills as possible, but that morning he sensed clear guidance to take a different, more difficult path.

Even as he walked, the bombing began. He broke into a run, the incessant noise drowning out the scuff of his own footsteps. Then one bomb fell nearby. Watching as he ran, Samuel realized it had struck the spot where he would have been walking if he had selected his usual route. Joy came to his heart and he praised God aloud. God was teaching him to be confident, whatever his circumstances.

By Christmas Day all of Hong Kong lay in the complete control of the conqueror. Ferry boats resumed their schedules. Samuel returned to Cheung Chou for a joyful reunion with his mother and sisters. "We prayed for you constantly," his mother told him. "We knew the angels would look after you."

With the Japanese in control and normal life impossible, Samuel's mother decided they should return to China, to Zhao Qing, where an uncle conducted a medical practice.

Again Samuel's family witnessed the power of faith. They traveled by boat up the bay and into the Pearl River, four boats together. On the second night, river pirates attacked. They boarded and pillaged three of the boats, but the boat on which Samuel's family traveled sailed on unharmed.

Samuel Lamb was being prepared for a future that would require the fullest measure of a man's faith, the deepest trust in God's promises.

4

IT WAS 1942. As the congregation gathered for morning worship at the Baptist church in Wuzhou, eighteen-year-old Samuel Lamb sat at the piano. With sure fingers and a melodious heart, he played an excerpt of the "Ode to Joy" from Beethoven's *Ninth Symphony*. On the platform, the missionary pastor kept time with his foot and studied his sermon notes. The missionary's wife, seated in one of the front pews, touched a small handkerchief to her eye. Pastor and wife, together with their colleagues, sensed potential in the young man. While Samuel studied at the Alliance Bible Institute in their city, he had chosen their church as his place of worship. Although he was not yet twenty, he quickly became one of the more resourceful and valuable members of the congregation.

While Samuel was in Wuzhou, he grew in several important ways. He practiced his piano skills at the home of the missionary hospital's chief of staff. He also studied English with the pastor, interpreting for him when he spoke to undergraduates at a nearby university. This experience helped to expand Samuel's vocabulary, especially in pulpit terminology.

To assist the many people displaced by the war, the Baptist missionaries built a colony of refugee huts in a corner of their compound. They offered one of the units to Samuel and his mother. She became a vendor at the hospital and was also an active member of the congregation.

Although accommodations were more basic than the family had known in Hong Kong, Samuel and his mother took a positive view. They knew their Good Shepherd was caring for his sheep, showing them how surely they could look to him in all circumstances. Later, his two sisters joined them, but his father remained at his teaching responsibilities in Singapore.

During those student days Samuel memorized large segments of Scripture, including the Epistles from Romans to Hebrews as well as many psalms and portions of John's gospel. His mother noticed his new interest and encouraged him. "You have not before given so much effort to Scripture memorization. God bless you, my son!"

"It will help me when I'm at last able to deliver sermons of my own," Samuel told his mother. He became reflective, adding, "When I see others in the pulpit, when I try to imagine myself in their place, I wonder what sort of preacher I could ever become."

"You will preach, Samuel, following your father's good example. Keep your heart warm, your spirit humble. Good preachers are like sponges, saturated with God's Word."

Young and immature though he was as a first-year Bible student, Samuel received his opportunity to stand at a pulpit much sooner than he had expected. One Sunday afternoon as he sat at the piano in the home of the missionary doctor, Samuel lightly explored one of Beethoven's sonatas. The doctor and his wife had gone to their field council and had given Samuel permission to use their living room while they were gone.

A knock summoned the student to the door. When he opened it, Samuel found the church's senior elder. "Your mother said I would find you here," he began. "A pedicab boy brought us a message from Brother Tao. He is ill and can't take the service tonight. We have spoken with the headmaster at the Alliance school. He informs us you have presented messages at the Bible Institute. Therefore, since you worship at our church, the elders have chosen you to give the evening sermon."

Samuel's mouth went paper-dry. He stood mute. "I've never preached to a congregation in a church," he reminded his mother as he discussed the fearful assignment with her.

"You must start sometime," she said kindly. "Tonight is the Lord's choice for you to begin."

Samuel selected his text from the opening verses of John 13, a passage he had been memorizing. Using what he had been learning in his elementary homiletics class, he constructed an outline. He cried to the Lord for guidance, totally without confidence and very afraid.

As he sat on the church platform that evening, he remembered the streets of Hong Kong, where an inner voice had rebuked his thought of pursuing wealth. Was it now the same voice scoffing at his presumption of one day following in the footsteps of his father?

He glanced at the piano. He had come to Wuzhou to prepare for the ministry. Might it, however, be the ministry of church music?

When time came for the sermon, Samuel's heart pounded. His thoughts went awhirl, and his lungs surged so wildly that he breathed like a person who had run a great distance and now must speak. At the pulpit, in full view of the audience, his mind went blank, and his tongue lay paralyzed in his mouth.

The congregation stirred, some appearing amused, others passing disdainful looks. Then he saw his mother, serene in the pew. She bowed her head.

Samuel took a deep breath. He opened his Bible and fumbled with the notes he had prepared. He once more looked at his mother. She finished her prayer, raised her head, fixed her eyes on her son, and smiled.

"In John 13," he began, "Jesus washes the feet of his disciples. We will note, in verse 5, that he poured the water, washed their feet, and dried them. That is to say, he did the total work of cleansing." Samuel looked back to his notes.

They confused him. Had he not in those introductory words delivered his whole sermon? What else was there to say?

Struggling, at times repeating himself, trying to follow his notes, he delivered his brief message. It lasted no longer than fifteen minutes.

When Samuel and his mother reached their little home, Samuel lamented, "I'll never be able to preach!"

"You preached tonight," his mother countered. "You preached the Word. Your father learned in his earliest sermons that God does not ask for performance but for faithful proclamation."

The tone of her voice became gentler. "To be sure, my dear son, you lacked eloquence tonight. That will come. But as you spoke, difficult as it was for you, I sensed unction. Only the Holy Spirit can give that to us. Never forget. Only the Holy Spirit gives unction. And tonight your mother witnessed the touch of God on her son. Mark it, Samuel. In my heart I know what I say is true."

At the beginning of Samuel's second year in Wuzhou, Bible Institute students learned of his proficiency with clipper and scissors. Many of them came to Samuel for haircuts. He continued his music studies and had several other opportunities to preach.

"You are not yet twenty," his mother encouraged. "You are making steady progress."

If learning to preach were dependent upon academic training, however, Samuel Lamb never would have succeeded because, as the Christmas holidays neared, news came of an aggressive Japanese army thrust southward.

One day the resident missionary called Samuel to his home. In the absence of Samuel's own father, the doctor and the pastor became like Samuel's relatives. "Our embassy advises us to leave," the missionary said. "Chiang Kai-Shek and Mao Zedong are attempting some kind of coalition, but lions and tigers never occupy the same lair. The Japanese seem to be grasping this opportunity to conquer all of China.

For missionaries to remain would surely be more harmful than helpful to our Chinese brothers and sisters."

"You will return?" the student asked. At this point in Samuel's life, the church and missionary presence were synonymous.

"When Chiang and Mao go for each other's throats, as many predict they will . . ." The missionary turned away.

As the two said good-bye to each other at the door, the missionary placed an envelope into Samuel's hand. Earlier as the mother had led her son and daughters in morning devotions, she had reminded them of special need to claim God's promises. "We have scarcely enough provisions should it be necessary to flee," she had said, "and not enough money to purchase tickets." The envelope Samuel brought home contained eight hundred dollars!

"The missionaries are not sure they will return," Samuel said to his family at the evening meal. "They have been good to us, helping us."

"They are our brothers and sisters," Samuel's mother said, "and brothers and sisters share—but it is God who provides our needs by whatever means he chooses, to whomever's heart he speaks."

Conditions worsened. Word came that unless disintegrating government forces could detain them, the Japanese army would reach Wuzhou in a few days. Hastily gathering their belongings, Samuel's family boarded a boat to take refuge in a village a few hours away, a site not likely to be of any importance in Japanese military strategy.

Samuel's mother and sisters set up a street stand, offering women's and children's dresses, which they made at night or purchased from refugee women. They kept hoping the crisis would blow over and they would be able to return to Wuzhou. But the Japanese not only captured Wuzhou from government forces, but also made the city their garrison for military advancement.

Again the family had no choice but to move on, coming to the village of Panghua. It seemed distinctly out of the Japanese thrust. Samuel once again became a barber, and his mother and sisters improvised a stand for dress sales.

Panghua turned out to be not only a haven for displaced people but also a hideout for local bandits.

Moving frequently to keep out of Japanese range, the family came to one city the day after it had been almost decimated by bombs and artillery. Again the Lord had safely ordered their steps.

By 1945, peace with Japan had come, and the family returned to Guangzhou and lived at the home of Samuel's grandfather. Here again Samuel sensed divine guidance, for the old man—long returned now from his earlier residence in Detroit—was under much duress.

Although Samuel's grandfather was a loyal churchman and a professing Christian, he needed assurance of salvation. Ignoring the Chinese tradition whereby young people do not advise older people, Samuel shepherded his grandfather to confident faith in the Savior.

He also visited his father, who had returned from Singapore to pastor a Baptist congregation in Hong Kong. His father strongly encouraged him to enter the ministry, but Samuel Lamb's musical talent again surfaced in Guangzhou. He gave concerts and became proficient in the compositions of Beethoven, Handel, Schubert, Mozart, and others. As a result, Samuel was asked to provide lessons for secondary school students. He wondered if the Lord was leading him into music after all.

During that time a position opened at Guangzhou's large Zion Church, then a Methodist congregation. The pastor was a fine evangelical and taught Samuel many things. Listening to him preach, Samuel found himself becoming more and more convinced that in spite of his feelings of inadequacy, God wanted him also to be a clergyman one day.

Zion Methodist Church figured into the life of Samuel Lamb, a Baptist, in a way he had not anticipated. The bishop installed a new pastor—a declared liberal. The new pastor and Samuel clashed from the outset.

"I have no choice but to leave the church," Samuel told his mother.

"If your choice results from obeying the Lord," his mother responded, "then you have no other option."

Samuel continued giving piano lessons. He taught a home class in English conversation. He also assisted in the ministry of a Baptist congregation and published a limited-edition hymnal.

"I hear more and more talk of some kind of restriction for churches," he told his mother one day. "In the North, some Christians are worshiping in homes." As her son spoke, the mother looked around at their quarters, spacious in comparison to many homes. In the late spring of 1950, Samuel Lamb began his own congregation, a house church with an initial membership of thirty communicants.

Later, during a visit to Hong Kong, he was called in for an interview at a prominent evangelical seminary. "Several of us are aware of your experience and proficiency in church music," the dean told him. The seminary offered Samuel a position that paid three times the salary he had earned at Zion Church. But what about the growing congregation that was meeting at his home? Should he accept the opportunity to minister through church music or should he continue as preacher in a small house church? In the end, Samuel refused the seminary's offer and could not be dissuaded. The decision to remain with the house church was to have grave implications for Samuel.

Upon returning to Guangzhou, Samuel was invited to speak at a church in the city of Fushan, two hours by train from Guangzhou. Sing Yin, a registered nurse and eighth daughter of a prominent medical doctor in the city, attended the service. She was introduced to the visiting speaker, Samuel Lamb. When Samuel met her, he knew she was God's choice for him. She sensed the same guidance in her life.

On July 4, 1951, they became husband and wife.

5

FOLLOWING THE CHINESE CUSTOM, Samuel took his bride into his family's home. She made herself kinfolk from the outset. Her new sisters-in-law loved her, and their mother, for all her matriarchal ways, found the newcomer suitable in temperament and spiritual qualities. Samuel affectionately called his spouse *Sui Ling*.

Sui Ling became an important part of their house-church ministry and especially encouraged Samuel in his preaching. "I received much blessing from your sermon," she would say.

Their love grew like a vine of the Lord's own planting and became in itself a ministry to others. When Samuel chided her for being so altruistic and helpful to him, she quoted one of the ancient sayings, "The king speaks of his wife as 'my royal lady,' while the queen speaks of herself as 'the king's handmaid.'"

Late one afternoon several months after their wedding, the young minister returned home from making some calls. His wife caught his hand and drew him into a quiet nook of the family dwelling. "We're going to have a baby," she told him simply.

The announcement came to Samuel's heart like airs of Beethoven, Mozart, and Handel in one composite crescendo. "Are you sure?" he asked.

"I am sure," she replied mirthfully, "and the doctor is certain."

"Sui Ling!" he whispered. "My Sui Ling!"

She was like a bar of hardest steel wrapped in swathing of softest wool—fortress and shelter to his mind and emotions—the helpmate God had given him. Now she was to be the mother of the wondrous being nestled in the cradle of her heart.

During the following months as Samuel played Bach's "Jesu, Joy of Man's Desiring" or a Grieg adagio on the piano, he tried to visualize the coming child, flesh of his own, fruit of his love for the one whom he looked after with pampering affection. "Don't be so concerned," Sui Ling chided, "or you will become the one who needs a doctor."

At last the baby arrived—a son. But the child lived only a scant thirty-three hours.

"O God!" Samuel cried out. "Why?" He later would learn to leave unsaid such questioning of divine wisdom. The Sovereign One had full right to give or take away. To question his ways was to doubt his words. Old Testament Abraham had written: "Will not the Judge of all the earth do right?" (Gen. 18:25)

"A Chinese father wishes his firstborn to be a son," Sui Ling comforted, struggling to dry her own tears. "But think how wondrous to know so surely we will meet him in heaven!"

In March of the following year, Sui Ling gave birth to a daughter, whom they named Hannah. Enoch was born the day after Christmas in 1954.

Before Enoch's birth Samuel had journeyed to Beijing for his first meeting with China's eminent clergyman Wang Mingdao. As he observed the ministry of Pastor Wang and saw him preach to his large congregation, a breath of wonder came to young Samuel's heart. Might the Lord ever give him such a ministry?

"Days of great testing lie ahead," Wang Mingdao cautioned. "Our faith and our faithfulness will be put to the weight of their fullest measure." At the time neither man suspected the accuracy of that prediction.

The Beijing visit increased Samuel's awareness of the suffering of Christians in China's northern provinces. He learned of one young pastor who had refused a power-crazed cadre's orders to stop preaching, and was crucified in the village market square. At dawn the pastor's anguished father, seeing his son still alive, ran to the foot of the cross. On his knees and weeping, he begged one of the soldiers standing guard to have mercy on his son. The soldier shot the old man, who died instantly.

Samuel learned of a widowed school teacher who had staunchly resisted demands to abandon classroom Bible readings and Christian teaching. She was tied by her long black hair to the back of a jeep and dragged back and forth in front of the school. Then her tormentors poured gasoline onto her torn body and threw on her a lighted match. She died—a living torch. The courageous teacher's twelve-year-old son, who was forced to watch the brutality, boldly reaffirmed his own personal faith.

Samuel learned of affluent Christians who refused flight to safety in Hong Kong before the complete communist take-over. One wealthy exporter insisted on staying in China and was ridiculed by his business colleagues. "I'm not leaving China," he told an American newsreporter. "When I witness to my staff of two hundred, they think I, too, will flee just before the Nationalists are overthrown. But I will stay. And when the communist occupation begins, I will have perhaps a brief time of golden opportunity to lead my people to the Savior!"

The exporter died of mistreatment in a labor camp. His wife, radiant in her faith, survived as a menial scrubwoman. Their mansion, their business complex—all of their possessions were confiscated.

Other Christians were buried alive, given the water cure, or kidnapped by army opportunists and held for ransom. Among those kidnapped was a Bible teacher who spent four months in a garret with a window too narrow for him to escape but wide enough to experience a miracle. Without a Bible, with no knowledge of his family or his impending fate, he asked God to give him some sign to assure him he was not forgotten. Within moments, a sparrow landed at the window, looked directly at him, and began to sing with shrill intensity. To make sure the bird had truly been sent as a minister to his need, the man paced back and forth. The bird turned its head back and forth to follow his movement. Then, as the Bible teacher dropped to his knees in gratitude to God, the sparrow completed its song and flew away. A few days later, with no explanation, the captive was set free.

All religious groups—Buddhists, Muslims, Christians—became targets of oppression. In desperation, many people renounced their beliefs, including some Christians, who were too frightened to identify with other believers.

The dust of the storm was rising. National holocaust loomed.

It is important to note that China (apart from the minorities) consists of two nations: North and South. The North is unified by modification of one language, Mandarin; the South is a cluster of entities, each with its own distinct dialect. Foreign influence from the ports of Hong Kong and Macau permeated much of the South, while the North remained staunchly Chinese, unified by the entrenched traditions of five millenia.

Just before the mid-century fall of Chiang Kai-Shek, inflation swept the land. The South, although by no means stable, enjoyed a measure of prosperity. Opportunists made a business of flying to Shanghai and Beijing with carry-on cases of U.S. currency and Chinese silver coins. These they exchanged for local paper currency at double-and-more the inflated rates and then returned to the South to reap benefits on the black market.

The new leadership met with a certain amount of disdain in urban centers like Guangzhou. Many of the cadres came from the Hunan province, known for its unsophisticated manners and amusingly accented speech.

The new revolutionary government disdained intelligentsia and determined to turn China into a scantly educated workers' paradise. Educators were dispatched to demeaning communes, eventually leaving the nation with one-hundred-fifty million illiterates.

Into this upheaval came the official church organization known as the Three-Self Patriotic Movement (TSPM), a self-governing, self-propagating, self-supporting organization. Oddly, TSPM, which was blatantly anti-foreign and anti-missionary, owed its conceptual origins to a European missionary who in 1851 saw the need for weaning China's Christians from dependence on outside support and leadership.

Although some TSPM clergymen were evangelical in theology and evangelistic in ministry, most found it difficult to minister under TSPM jurisdiction. Bishop Ding, head of the Three-Self organization, today was a former Anglican priest who had an alleged disdain for most evangelicals. In Three-Self's close identity with the atheistic authorities, clergymen were encouraged to omit sermon texts and topics involving Genesis, Revelation, and particularly the prophet Daniel. The atheistic view of human origin was evolutionary, with no tolerance for creationism. Furthermore, the new ideology promised a future utopia, not some fancied Parousia in which the Son of God would rend the skies and come to earth to establish his kingdom.

During those early days of transition and struggle, Samuel Lamb and his congregation came under close scrutiny from Three-Self. They knew Samuel had been associated with the Zion congregation, which later had associated with Three-Self. They also knew Samuel had left Zion Church in protest and had established a house church.

While many people remained in Three-Self and tried to maintain their personal convictions, thousands of other Christians all over China began attending house churches rather than identify with TSPM's strong liberal bias. In retaliation against the exodus of Three-Self communicants, house churches where more than thirty-five people assembled were declared illegal. Attendance at the Lamb family residence at 35 Da Ma Zhan soon exceeded thirty-five.

In the early months of 1955, lack of cooperation with Three-Self became synonymous with resistance to the government. The government began a national cleanup movement to rid the nation of anti-government dissidents.

"Sooner or later," Samuel told his wife, "we will be included. I have warned our co-workers to be ready."

"Ready?" Sui Ling asked. Her voice was taut but not fearful.

Samuel only smiled and nodded his head. His wife understood. She helped him pack a small bundle with changes of clothes. At the next worship service Samuel tactfully warned his congregation that he might be leaving them soon. Sui Ling lifted the edge of a kerchief to her eyes but did not weep.

One day in early August Samuel returned from calling on members of the house church. His wife met him at the door and showed him the early evening newspaper. A front-page heading read: LEADING DISSIDENT ARRESTED. Samuel skimmed the article quickly and learned that his loved and respected friend Wang Mingdao had been jailed, and awaited trial.

The following Sunday, the Da Ma Zhan pastor took his text from Hebrews 11, the "faith chapter," emphasizing the last nine verses, which recounted those who had suffered for their faithfulness. Some had faced jeers and flogging, while still others had been put in prison. They had been stoned; they had been sawed in two; they had been put to death by the sword. They had gone about in sheepskins and goatskins, destitute, persecuted, and mistreated—the world had not been worthy of them.

Within the following month, congregation members Sister Mei Feng Zhu and Brother Lee Hong Sun, both educators at a Guangzhou university, were simultaneously arrested. "The Communists have a special hatred for intellectuals," Samuel reminded his wife when he returned home one afternoon. "And those who preach the Gospel are numbered among them."

It was too tense a situation for levity. Instead, Samuel sighed and added, "I suppose I should feel honored, a humble preacher of the Gospel being thought of as an intellectual."

Sui Ling smiled, although her husband had not. "Just this morning," she said, "as I was reading in Isaiah, I came upon these verses: 'Fear not, for I have redeemed you; I have called you by name; you are mine.'" She took her husband's coat. "'When you pass through the waters, I will be with you . . . for I am the LORD, your God, the Holy One of Israel, your Savior.'"

It was the evening of September 14, 1955, a Wednesday. The Da Ma Zhan congregation would be gathering for Bible study and prayer. Sui Ling escorted her dear husband to the table, hurried to the kitchen, and brought food she had kept warm for him. "Many pastors have been arrested," Samuel said, more a statement than an indication of his own apprehension. "They have these kangaroo trials. I'm told Christians themselves testify against each other to save their own necks." Samuel touched the food with his chopsticks, lifted a morsel partly from the bowl but did not take it to his mouth.

"Don't be afraid, Samuel."

He did not immediately respond. He looked instead into Sui Ling's eyes, saw the uncertainty there, and began eating.

"I do wonder at times," he admitted. He paused again and reached to touch his wife's hand.

"I'm prepared to face whatever comes," Sui Ling said.

"Some pastors are being tortured, even put to death."

"But only in the North?" Sui Ling asked, remaining poised.

"I don't know," Samuel responded quietly. Changing the subject, he added, "House churches are growing everywhere. We here at Da Ma Zhan are part of a great body the Lord is raising up to honor his name in China." He hesitated, pondering, and added, "Perhaps for an outreach and ingathering such as China has never seen before."

A special glory descended over the Bible study and intercession time an hour later. The arrest of Mei Feng Zhu and Lee Hong Sun stimulated rather than hindered attendance.

"People on the street look at us strangely when we come for our meetings," said one brother. "It seemed even more so tonight."

"I do not get the impression," said another, "that they hold offense against us."

"To the contrary!" voiced a third. "I detect a look of envy in the eyes of some. We must always show, even in our public manner, the joy we have in Christ."

Their pastor reminded them, "Paul told the Corinthians that we are the aroma of Christ." He told them to think of themselves as epistles known and read by everybody. Opening his Bible to 2 Corinthians, he added, "You show that you are a letter from Christ . . . written not with ink but with the Spirit of the living God, not on tablets of stone but on tablets of human hearts."

Following the Bible study, Samuel and Sui Ling invited staff members to linger for tea and fellowship. Discussion was crisp, held to muffled sounds.

"We can never thank God enough for your ministry, Pastor Lamb," Wang Gao Xian commented. "You prepare us for joy, not sorrow."

"Consider it pure joy," Samuel quoted James 1, "whenever you face trials. . . ."

Zhang Yao Sheng, another staff member, added, "The testing of your faith develops perseverance."

Sui Ling brought tea. Brother Wang said as he sipped, "You know exactly how long to boil the water, Sister Lamb, and precisely when to add the leaves."

"Perchance tonight she added tears," a woman in the group said. Sui Ling managed a wan smile, then retreated to another part of the flat.

At 10:00 o'clock, without knocking, a group of people entered—several civilians and two policemen. *I wonder if they are from Three-Self?* Samuel Lamb thought. The strangers began searching the living quarters and took note of Samuel's bundle of belongings. They chattered among themselves until two of them, leafing through a photo album Sui Ling had been assembling, discovered a photograph of

Samuel and Wang Mingdao. Sui Ling came into the room and bravely stepped forward.

"That is mine," she said calmly, "pictures of interest only to our family."

"This is not family!" one of the visitors quipped. He pointed to the photograph. "This is subversive." The entire album was confiscated, and never returned.

The layman leading the group, like another Judas in a subsequent Gethsemane, gestured to Samuel, Mr. Wang, and Mr. Zhang.

Instantly, handcuffs appeared.

"It was an ugly experience," remembers Samuel. "It was the ultimate in losing face for a Chinese. I often wore handcuffs in times following my initial arrest, but this first time lingers most in my mind."

The three men were pushed toward the door.

"Oh!" Sui Ling gasped.

Samuel turned back to speak to her.

"Silence!" a policeman commanded. He turned Samuel toward the exit.

"It hurt me deeply," Samuel remembers, "being unable even to bid my dear wife good-bye!"

6

THE NEXT DAY, Sui Ling secured a copy of *Nan Fang Daily* and read the lead story, which stated:

> Anti-revolutionary activists, masterminded by a leading dissident posing as an illegal house-church pastor, were seized by police late last night and are being held for questioning.

"Merciful Lord," Sui Ling whispered. She had not slept all night. Neither had her husband.

Together with Mr. Wang and Mr. Zhang, Samuel Lamb had been taken to one of the government's detention centers for interrogation throughout the night. "You are an anti-revolutionary activist," he was told. "You are attempting to cover up major secrets. Your crime is seen as high among the threats against the government." The very tone of the man's voice made his words sound like recitation of guilt before a criminal was executed.

Resolute though he was in his faith, sure of God's constant and watchful care, some uneasy thoughts invaded Samuel's mind. Would the men be shot? Or hanged? Pushing out these uneasy thoughts were Scripture verses assuring Samuel that "whether by life or by death," the future was in God's hands, beyond the power of his oppressors.

At last, sometime after daybreak, the men were taken to their cells. They were not locked up together as they had wanted.

Samuel's cell stank from rancid fumes rising from a toilet bucket. The walls were stark, reminding him of a tomb. The motionless air, dank and acrid, wrapped around him like a serpent's coils.

Samuel thought he heard a volley of rifle shots but decided it was only his imagination. The sound occurred a second time—louder, closer—but Samuel assumed it to be vehicles backfiring.

Silently he committed himself to the One who said, "All things work together for good," and who told his followers, "Peace I leave with you; my peace I give you. I do not give to you as the world gives. Do not let your hearts be troubled and do not be afraid."

"Yes, Lord Jesus," he whispered. "Yes."

Just then from a distant cell, he heard singing. It was his two parishioners.

> To suffer is to serve our Lord.
> Our tears, like His, touch heaven.

From his cell, Samuel joined them.

> We are the children of His Word
> To whom all grace is given.

Never had so short a singing brought so abundant a blessing to the heart of Samuel Lamb.

Interrogation sessions continued night after night, especially for Samuel. The sessions usually began just before midnight and proceeded through the night. Officials in charge took turns in what prisoners came to know as "fatigue sessions."

One night in a momentary display of compassion, Samuel received a freshly boiled egg. Hungry from the inadequate prison diet, he ate the morsel with thanks to

God. Later that session, when Samuel was weary to the point of mental confusion, he was given a paper to read. Glancing at the contents, he saw it to be a "confession" of the false accusations made against him.

"Read it," his interrogator said. As Samuel immersed himself in the contents of the paper, the assistant placed a microphone in front of him.

"But these statements are untrue!" Samuel protested.

"I know," said the interrogator, gently like a friend, "but my superiors need a statement of the issues being considered in our sessions."

Samuel's mind was so weary that he could not find words to further his protest.

"You are tired," the gentle voice continued. "But before you take some rest, please read the statement. Read it aloud."

"But, sir—"

"This is not a formal hearing or legal proceeding, Mr. Lamb. So just read the statement and go to your rest. Request that we keep the recording confidential, and we will do it."

Hardly believing it was his own voice he heard, Samuel read.

On September 27, Three-Self leaders called a public accusation meeting against the Da Ma Zhan pastor. Despite all his misgivings about TSPM, he found it difficult to imagine a professed Christian agency stooping to such tactics against a declared believer. Three-Self made sure Samuel was not at the meeting.

However, members of the Da Ma Zhan congregation attended. Fellow Christians stood mute as the chairman asked for people to make accusations against Pastor Lamb. A man responded. "I am not a member of the Da Ma Zhan congregation," he said, "but I have attended many of the services out of curiosity. Samuel Lamb blatantly speaks out against the government, denouncing it as atheistic. He says all atheists are going to burn in a lake of fire and brimstone." The man was a total stranger to members of the congregation. None recalled ever seeing him at one of the services.

Other "accusers" followed, delivering what sounded suspiciously like scripted harangues.

In his cell Samuel Lamb was a man at peace, refreshing his mind and spirit with sustaining portions of God's Word, "He was oppressed and afflicted, yet he did not open his mouth; he was led like a lamb to the slaughter."

An elderly woman of the congregation was forced forward. As members watched, they remembered her face as she had often listened to Samuel Lamb preach at Da Ma Zhan. They remembered her eager eyes, her smile, her nods of approval at what she heard. Would she, in fear, speak negatively against her leader?

The chairman signaled for her to speak. "I have attended many of the preaching services and Bible studies," she began. "I have received much help. In the past, I knew nothing of the saving mercy of Christ. Pastor Lamb helped me—" The guards quickly led away the "uncooperative" woman.

When she had gone, a tape recording was played. It was a skillfully edited version of the supposedly confidential and harmless statement Samuel had been coerced into making.

Back in his cell the accused man realized these were definitive hours in his fate and ministry, yet the peace in his heart remained.

It was at this time that Samuel Lamb became so fully aware of the Presence. He turned to look, almost expecting to see someone. He saw nothing, but in not seeing, he became all the more aware. He thought he heard the Presence say, "He shall give his angels charge over thee, to keep thee in all thy ways."

Though the Presence startled him, he felt he could almost reach out and touch the reality. He had been aware of the Presence before in his life—but never so markedly as now.

Samuel began singing softly:

When we walk with the Lord,
In the light of His Word,
What a glory He sheds on our way!

There *was* a Presence. Not some fancied phantasm but a
tangible entity more visible to his spiritual eyes than to his
physical eyes.

Hallelujah!

The Presence reminded him, "Are not all angels
ministering spirits, sent to serve those who will inherit
salvation?" Praise the Lord of Lords! Exalted be his name
forever and ever! This awareness would follow Samuel
through the tense times awaiting him.

When Sundays came, Samuel wondered about his
congregation. Would they be too frightened to gather?
Would they assemble but devote the time to silent intercession? Would others of them be implicated?

Samuel was reminded of Paul's words written to the
Philippians from his prison cell: "Do not be anxious about
anything, but in everything, by prayer and petition, with
thanksgiving, present your requests to God. And the peace
of God, which transcends all understanding, will guard your
hearts and your minds in Christ Jesus."

He went to his hard steel bed and knelt. "My wife may
not know where I am," he prayed quietly. "My mother may
not know. My people. But you know, my Jesus, and I can be
strong and secure in—"

A guard banged loudly on the bars of the cell. Samuel
looked up. "You!" the guard bellowed. "You sick?"

"No, sir."

"The warden has no time for them that pretends sick,
and there's not a brush's stroke to be gained if you do."

The prisoner arose and sat on the edge of his bed. The
guard stalked on.

The confines of his cell, the uncertainty surrounding
him, his total isolation from those he loved and to whom he
ministered—everything lay totally outside his frame of faith.
In these early hours of his first detention Samuel Lamb
experienced a spiritual and physical sensation that would

remain with him as a part of his very anatomy for the remainder of his life.

Peace!

The stink of the prison and the stifling air became subdued realities compared to the breath of divine assurance that permeated his being. The emotion was multidimensional—living in his spirit while at the same time radiating through organs and flesh, muscles and marrow, to relax his body and bolster his morale. Through his mind echoed the promises, *My peace I give you. I do not give to you as the world gives. . . . We share in his sufferings in order that we may also share in his glory.*

"Be it so, Lord," he whispered. "Make me willing. Show me how to accept."

Within the hour Samuel heard singing. It was a male voice from some other area of the prison. Farther away from where he had heard his parishioners, Gao Xian and Yao Sheng. "Onward Christian soldiers . . ."

Samuel waited for more. "Onward Christian soldiers . . ." the man repeated.

"Marching as to war," Samuel sang in return, and waited.

"With the cross of Jesus . . ." the refrain continued.

Samuel added, "Going on before!"

"Prisoner!" it was the same guard again. "You don't sing in here!"

"Christ the Royal Master . . ." came from the distance. Samuel dared not respond. "Christ the Royal Master . . ." was repeated.

Then all was silent. Samuel never again heard the joyous antiphonal.

The experience once again taunted his distress at not being able to sit at a piano. Yet, in his fantasies he played Beethoven, Mozart, Schubert. Once he imagined himself playing the entire score of the *Messiah*.

During his Guangzhou imprisonment, Samuel wrote several of the hymns that later appeared in his *Voices in the Wilderness* hymnal: "Be Humble," "Know Yourself," and "We Need Revival."

One of the hymns, "Dismantling Before Rebuilding," probed deeply into his struggling years of spiritual growth. Samuel composed the music in summer, the words in early autumn.

> *My walk with Christ had but begun.*
> *My lamp of love for Him burned low.*
> *Then His love, like the morning sun,*
> *Set my weak wick of faith aglow!*

As he quietly sang his hymns, they were transformed from his compositions into heavenly melodies sent down to bless his soul. Just as the beloved apostle had his prison epistles, the beloved pastor would have his prison hymns.

December 18, 1955, over three months after he had been arrested, Samuel was transferred to a second detention center on Cangbian Road in Guangzhou. As he watched the other detainees assemble in the yard, he saw his two parishioners, Wang Gao Xian and Zhang Yao Sheng. His first impulse was to call out to them, but guards permitted no conversation, not even whispers.

As the believers caught sight of each other, Samuel gestured heavenward. The two parishioners nodded and smiled. Joy came to their faces as they fellowshiped in those precious moments of silence. It was a nonverbal sermon from pastor to parishioners.

In the second detention center, Samuel was placed with some forty other prisoners in a cramped room. He slept on the floor alongside a Catholic priest, who said, "It is my honor to meet you. The name Samuel Lamb has been discussed among the priests of our diocese. We respect your courage and integrity."

Weeks faded into months through the lingering winter, on into spring and early summer. The long days of inactivity and uncertainty wore heavily on the prisoners.

"Will they leave us here to rot?" one man asked.

"Like bodies in a common grave?" wondered another.

Samuel became his own teacher in those days, a pastor to himself. One of the sermons lingering in his thoughts might have been titled: "Our Multi-Faceted Faith." In the pleasant places of life, in times of certainty and security, God's children deepen their trust and spiritual awareness only through strictest discipline. But when darkness comes, when life's basics are shaken by threats and disasters, then the King's children most clearly recognize their pilgrim status. That's when faith seeks out the deepest terrains of Scripture.

From his store of memorized books, chapters, and verses, Samuel drew out promises and perceptions he had never thought about before. "I have learned to be content whatever the circumstances," Paul had told the Philippians. Samuel could paraphrase those words and say, "I am *learning* to be content."

To the strum of his instrument, the psalmist had sung, "Delight yourself in the LORD and he will give you the desires of your heart." The promise was not for the fulfillment of personal desires. Rather, a yielded heart opens its doors and windows to the Sovereign One and invites him to plant the *desires* that will in turn invoke prayers and actions harmonious with his will.

Time stood all but still those torturous days, yet the Presence remained. Scripture did its cleansing and fulfilling work, and Samuel Lamb was a man at peace.

On May 22, 1956, Samuel was transferred back to the first detention site. Once again the Good Shepherd ordained an inspiring and comforting meeting. Samuel was handcuffed in tandem with Sister Mei Feng Zhu from the Da Ma Zhan congregation.

"Be not afraid," the saintly woman said quietly.

"God is with us," Samuel responded.

That was the sum of their fellowship. They soon were separated again. The Presence had arranged this moment of encouragement.

With excruciating slowness, the time passed. Those prison months had few routines. Because Samuel had been given no sentence, he had no tasks, and few privileges—only day after day and night after night of uncertainty.

The cell had three beds. Two more prisoners joined

Samuel. One of them, Liang Shu Dong, had heard vaguely about the Gospel.

"You play chess?" the other prisoner asked one day.

"I have played," Samuel replied.

On the guards' next round, the prisoner asked for a chess board. The request was granted, but Samuel played only a few games. As a Hong Kong schoolboy he had been runner-up in an all-colony chess tournament. So when he won every match, the other prisoner lost interest and returned the chess board to a passing guard.

Samuel spent hours studying Scripture verses he had memorized. Passages he thought he had forgotten surfaced as clearly as if he had recently memorized them.

The Presence remained, and in Samuel's heart grew an all-encompassing peace. He held tightly to the promise, "I can do all things through Christ which strengtheneth me."

Samuel's heart grew increasingly burdened for Shu Dong, the more receptive of his two cellmates. Samuel knew he must not overtly witness to the man because aggressive witnessing anywhere in China, especially if one was already behind bars, could result in serious consequences. Samuel prayed instead that Shu Dong himself would open the door.

It happened one morning after the other cellmate was taken for interrogation. "I watch you," Shu Dong said. "Your face is never sad."

"That's because I have Christ's joy in my heart," Samuel told him.

"Are you religious because you fear a firing squad?"

"First, I'm not religious. Life in Christ is very different from mere religion. Second, I do not anticipate death, but I don't fear it either. The Bible teaches that 'to live is Christ and to die is gain.'"

That morning the drab confines of a cell in Guangzhou Prison became a sanctuary as Liang Shu Dong's name entered the pages of the Book of Life.

Typical of converts in China, the new believer became insatiably hungry to know more. He and Samuel sat by the hour in a quiet corner of the cell, Shu Dong asking questions, the pastor responding. They conversed in low voices to avoid surveillance and to avoid irritating their cellmate, who became curious and would listen to them for long periods of time.

"Do you hold all of the Bible in your mind?" he asked late one night as the three lay on their beds, "or do you compose those quotations and trick us into thinking they are God's Word, as you say?"

"I quote the Bible as accurately as I can remember it," Samuel told him.

"I was once skeptical as well," said Shu Dong, "but now my heart is washed clean with truth. You, too, can experience this."

Just then a guard beat lightly on the bars of the cell. "No talking after lights are out!" he warned.

It was the last time the third prisoner expressed interest in the Gospel. The spirit of Liang Shu Dong, however, grew like a nurtured plant. The two men sang together the new hymns Samuel had written, and their cellmate did not protest.

One day without any announcement, Shu Dong was removed from the cell. "He has blabbed religion to the wrong felon," the cellmate surmised, "and has taken a bullet to his gut." He added, "I will hear no more of your ideas. All I am interested in is getting out of this place."

Faithfully but cautiously, Samuel continued to witness to other men in the detention center. Many listened, but fear hindered them from accepting his message. Samuel never spoke to guards. They seemed to be a remote species—automatons, puppets on strings. At times Samuel felt like a free man compared to the guards, who were held captive by an oppressive system.

Samuel also began hearing reports of executions of offenders put to death on the day of arrest. He had no way of knowing whether the reports were true or just rumors. It troubled him that when prisoners assembled in the outside yard, he saw nothing of Shu Dong or members of the Da Ma Zhan congregation.

When Ai Ling came to visit her brother, she spoke of increasing numbers of accusation posters appearing on the walls of Da Ma Zhan street. Many, she said, had check marks at the bottom, indicating executions. "Your poster is hung at the doorway to our place," she said. When Samuel asked for more detail, a guard announced that their visit was over.

Prison conditions worsened. Officials became more insensitive to prisoners' needs; the rice and vegetables became less palatable. Samuel wondered if there had been a change of air in the cell block since the day he was incarcerated.

A prisoner would sometimes go berserk in the dead of night, screaming and banging the bars with his fists and head. One prisoner threw his waste bucket against the cell door, spewing wretched excrement onto the outer floor and into opposite cells. He was taken away.

At times like this, Samuel most assuredly sensed the Presence. Peace filled the deepest recesses of his mind and heart. Words of Scripture emerged from his memory to appear with emblazoned brush strokes on the walls of his mind. He could accept whatever the Shepherd permitted to come his way.

As Samuel lay on his cot one afternoon, reviewing Scriptures and praying, his cell door opened. "Prisoner Lamb!" a guard announced curtly.

The uncertainty of the moment caught Samuel unprepared. Was this termination for him? Would a check be placed at the bottom of his poster on the Da Ma Zhan walls?

The Presence whispered, "All things work together for good to them that love God." Samuel knew it to be true.

7

WHEN SAMUEL LAMB WALKED out of his cell at Guangzhou Prison on January 28, 1957—after nearly a year and a half of detention—he was not so much a free man as an alleged culprit. His enemies wanted to inflict censorship on him, but they could find no cause. He was neither acquitted nor proved guilty.

When Samuel stepped off the bus at Zhong Shan 5 and entered the ancient gateway to Da Ma Zhan street, shopkeepers and neighbors observed in wonder. Everyone had expected Samuel Lamb, the courageous pastor, either to be put to death for his disobedience or sentenced to long imprisonment.

Some people greeted him. Others stared in disbelief. Most watched in silent curiosity.

Sui Ling recognized her beloved's approaching footsteps and bounded to the door, and the children followed. "God answers prayer!" his mother exclaimed. His sisters looked on and wept.

Samuel knew, of course, how difficult it would be not to cause further offense. Members of his congregation who had relatives and friends elsewhere in China relayed incidents of government and Three-Self oppression of the rebellious *xiao-xu*, as small groups were called.

House churches not only were ordered closed but their members also were warned of dire penalties if they reassembled. Yet house-church ministry continued. When pastors or lay leaders were arrested, wives assumed responsibilities.

In one case, while a pastor went to labor camp for leading a *xiao-zu*, his wife established a tea shop at the front of their dwelling. She charged break-even prices, so customers thronged the establishment nightly, providing excellent cover for services held at the rear of the second floor above.

When officials suspected activity at one residence, they dispatched a policeman to investigate. He remained through a service and at the conclusion came to a personal and decisive relationship with the Son of God.

All over China disgruntled members of Three-Self congregations sought out house churches for more vital preaching and teaching. In one instance, church officials appointed five staunch TSPM adherents to spy on a group in their area. Even though the five people came as spies, they were captivated by the vitality of the singing and preaching. As a result, the five spies embraced the message and committed themselves to Jesus Christ!

Even though missionaries had been forced out of China, its Christian population had multiplied through personal evangelism, ninety percent of which was done by laypeople. Christians won their friends and associates and then brought them to church for instruction and inspiration. The new believers, many of whom had been raised as atheists, rarely had any knowledge whatever of Scripture.

After a brief rest at Sui Ling's parental home, Samuel returned to ministry. He found that the restrictions had not relaxed, but that the Guangzhou officials tended to look the other way. TSPM interferences also seemed to be less regular.

"How good it is to have a pastor again!" exclaimed Sister Mei who, along with Mr. Wang and Mr. Zhang, had been released several months earlier. The three immediately became active in the thriving congregation.

Samuel tried to forget his time in prison, but with the passing of each day he became increasingly curious. For what cause had he been arrested? Having been neither acquitted nor proved guilty, he decided to inquire.

"As a citizen," he spoke to one official, "I feel I have the right to ask why I was arrested and held without charge or explanation."

The official vaguely responded, "I can only suggest that earlier it was a matter of anti-revolution, whereas now it is problems with the peasantry." Samuel did not understand this response, but he decided not to press for clarification.

Samuel wondered how he had escaped execution. Why hadn't a check mark appeared below his posted record on the walls of Da Ma Zhan? Did the Presence oversee his affairs? Did an angel maneuver the documents of his case, passing them through the hands of those who understood that the law should protect citizens as well as punish criminals? He could only affirm that every child of God striving to be in his will is immortal until his work is finished.

Not that all had suddenly become tranquillity and bliss. TSPM officials kept an obviously watchful eye on Samuel Lamb's activities. A TSPM representative came openly one day and talked to Samuel about the possibility of being placed in a Three-Self pulpit. He tried to picture for Samuel the large opportunities he could have in the ministry of an official church.

"Would this mean I could preach the Bible as I believe it, uplifting the Lord God as the Creator, depicting Jesus Christ as Savior and soon-coming King?" The representative said nothing and immediately left.

The Da Ma Zhan congregation grew to more than one hundred, often suspecting that observers from Three-Self were in the audience. To avoid consequent censure, Samuel rarely mentioned money in his preaching and teaching. Seasoned church members understood the principles of tithing and practiced conscientious stewardship. Many of them earned little more than subsistence salaries, however, and had only a little to give. Others, students and new believers, could not give or had not yet added tithing to their agenda of spiritual obedience and discipleship. The pastor's salary was thus sporadic and minimal.

Sui Ling, a graduate nurse, looked for work. Wherever she went, however, her husband's prison record followed her. Also she lacked an approved *danwei* (the work unit or governmental group to which one reports). As Samuel and Sui Ling retired to their room one night, Sui Ling said, "Your mother manages the household well and she is always accepting of me. I realize, though, that she senses the pressure of our limited finances."

"I could teach English classes again," Samuel suggested.

"But that would limit your effectiveness as a pastor." Sui Ling took a deep breath. "When I last visited my father in Fushan, he told me of the need for an additional nurse in his medical work. As a family member, I am part of his *danwei*."

Thus it was that Sui Ling moved to Fushan, returning on most weekends to Samuel and little Enoch. Hannah went to another relative.

Alone from Monday through Friday, Samuel devoted increasingly more time to Bible study. He did not strive for pulpit eloquence. His sermons were conversational in tone with increasing emphasis on scriptural content.

"You have such rich material, my son," his mother encouraged. "And to think you once wondered if you could ever occupy a pulpit! You supposed only orators could be preachers." In a more serious vein she added, "Do you ever think to put some of your best thoughts into writing? More people should benefit from your insights."

"But how would my work be published," he questioned, "with conditions as they are these days?"

"Times will change," the wise woman said.

Samuel had purchased a hand-operated mimeograph unit for making sermon notes available to his listeners. With the help of volunteers, he proceeded to develop seven booklets on major themes of the Christian faith. The popularity of the effort exceeded his expectations. Titles included: "The True

God," "The Lord Is Coming Soon," "The Holy Spirit and Christians," and "Is the Bible True?"

Zhu Quen, a middle-aged man in the congregation, was among the enthusiasts who not only read the books over and over for himself but secured copies for distribution. "I am only a simple man," Zhu Quen told his pastor, "with very little education. These books open my mind to truths I never realized or understood before."

The quiet man's words touched Samuel deeply. Zhu Quen was a laborer who fit the mold of Mao Zedong strategy, yet he was a man who witnessed boldly at the continual risk of his own security.

Through the summer months and early autumn of 1957, Samuel Lamb and his growing congregation ministered in a climate of considerable freedom. During such times, Christians all across China learned the art of silent witness as exemplary models. In factories, offices, campuses, and marketplaces emerged a lifestyle and value system that came to be known as Christian.

In one northern commune, a contingent of Christians found each other and proceeded to add converts to their number. A young cadre came on staff, a man eager to please his superiors. He would arrive early in the morning at the central area. He first would make sure his senior cadre had noticed his early arrival. Then with a confident swagger, he would look over the buildings in the section he would administer.

One day he entered a hay barn immediately adjacent to the fields. To his surprise, he came upon a group of Christians praying so intently that none of them detected his presence. He filled his lungs, ready to reprimand them, but he held back, realizing it would be much better to inform the senior cadre and thereby gain merit points.

"You didn't disturb them, did you?" the senior cadre flared when the young man announced his finding.

"No, sir," replied the upstart, disappointed and perplexed.

"Never trouble them."

"But—"

"They are the best workers we have."

As 1957 drew toward winter, Christians in many areas sensed rising tension. No single event caused it. There was no decree from Beijing, just a pervading mood and awareness.

"We need to pray more," Samuel Lamb counseled his staff. "And we must avoid taking unnecessary chances. Let us preach and teach what the Bible says about living for the glory of God. We need to avoid any reference to politics."

"Oh, yes," Sui Ling concurred, during one of her weekend visits. "Please don't take any chances. The situation is the same in Fushan. Christians fear an uproar at any moment."

Take no chances . . .

At the first of the year, Samuel was served notice to attend a nine-day Christian conference. He initially declined. "Will it hurt the work if you do not cooperate?" Sui Ling asked. "Might it be something you could attend in silence, offering no participation?" Samuel knew that his wife was completely supportive of his evaluation of Three-Self. He also knew and appreciated her astuteness.

When he made cautious inquiry, he was told that the conference involved only educational seminars. Samuel thought it might be important to attend. Several of his staff were wary, but Samuel eventually persuaded them to go with him at least to have a look.

Taking no chances was he?

The conference involved leaders from twenty-four former denominations, some who, like Samuel, had not yet linked pulpits with TSPM. Samuel realized that the group had a strong liberal bias and wondered if he should leave.

Almost as if he were their prime target, TSPM leaders set upon the pastor from 35 Da Ma Zhan, using various turns of alleged truth in an effort to persuade him to join forces with them. Surprising even himself, Samuel relented and convinced his staff as well to make their congregation a member of Three-Self. He believed they would be guaranteed freedom to preach the Gospel and teach the truths Christians needed for continuing growth.

To his consternation and amazement, the program director of the China Christian Council scheduled the playing of the tape of the confession that Samuel earlier had been tricked into making—but with all of the misleading untruths having been edited out.

Samuel and his staff were given the warm hand of fellowship!

8

THE WHEELS OF THREE-SELF ENCROACHMENT turned slowly. At first people thought Samuel was involved with TSPM but free to minister with a clear conscience. Samuel, however, was to be divinely hindered through a dreadful turn of events.

It happened one Friday evening after he and Enoch had gone to bed. Sui Ling was not at home; she was due to arrive the next morning from Fushan.

The night had been exceptionally calm—even Da Ma Zhan, which can be noisy at nightfall, settled down to an almost foreboding stillness. Samuel lay on his bed, lost in thought. In the moonlight coming through the window, he could see his cherished little son breathing quietly, and he wondered what the future held for his children. Would the family one day come together again, with mother, father, and siblings growing together as Christians and thriving in a climate of love and sharing?

He heard scuffling. Then he heard someone, his mother or sister, go to the door. He gave the noise no second thought. Then the light came on in his room and several blurred figures rudely entered. As his eyes grew accustomed to the sudden brightness, a policeman stepped to his bedside.

"You are under arrest," the policeman said. Another person held high a warrant. Enoch awakened and began to scream. His grandmother slipped into the room and took him away.

"Put on some clothes!" the intruder with the warrant commanded. Before Samuel could fully comply, he was handcuffed and led out of the dwelling. His mother and sisters watched from silent shadows.

"Our prayers are with you," he heard his mother say.

Only the Holy Spirit's ministration, no strength or virtue of his own, enabled Samuel to accept, without a fret or question, his return to Guangzhou Prison.

"Evil never triumphs when it comes on the children of God," his mother had told him. "The Lord always provides mercy in our suffering, strength for our weakness, grace to accept what we can't understand. The night of adversity must ever yield its darkness to the morning of blessing. I may not live to see it, my son, but however deeply Christians suffer in these times, a glorious morning is sure to dawn."

The prison cell differed only in its location, not in appearance. It gave off the same stench. It held the same acrid air. It looked like the same tomb.

The cell's other two inmates lay sleeping. So, as the clack of the guard's footsteps faded, Samuel knelt by the protruding slab that was to be his bed. "I trust in you, O LORD," he prayed, quoting a memorized psalm. "You are my God. My times are in your hands."

He stretched out on the bed and, in a whisper, sang.

> To suffer is to serve our Lord.
> Our tears, like His, touch Heaven.
> We are the children of His Word
> To whom all grace is given.

That special gloria returned full into his heart, and with it came an aura of confidence and peace. He did not sleep, but lay on his bed, quietly thinking about the goodness of a

God who could allow one of his children to be treated like
this and yet be so sure of his care and blessing.

We are the children of His Word
To whom all grace is given.

A guard came, replaced the handcuffs, and led him to a
waiting vehicle. Samuel was taken to the Justice Building of
Guangzhou, where he promptly was led into judicial
chambers.

"You have not learned your lesson," the judge reprimanded. He spoke more as a father to an errant son than as
an official of the court. "You were granted freedom, but you
persisted in disobeying the law. What if all Chinese were like
you? Think what chaos our nation would face."

Samuel stood silent.

"You are charged with being an anti-revolutionary and
a pro-imperialist," he continued, as if he were reading a
transcript from Samuel's earlier appearances at the tribunal
bench. "You collaborate with Wang Mingdao of Peking. You
are now anti-Russian."

Anti-Russian? Samuel thought. In the moment, Samuel
remembered a series of sermons he had recently preached
from Ezekiel 37 and 38, prophetic chapters about Israel under
attack by hordes from the North. Samuel also recalled that a
stranger had sat in the audience.

"How do you plead?" the judge asked crisply.

"Not guilty, Your Honor."

"If you will be cooperative," the judge said, fatherly
again in his tone of voice, "I can consider leniency for your
sentence."

"But I cannot plead guilty," Samuel said quietly,
"when I am innocent."

Angrily, the judge half-shouted, "Then I have no
alternative but to recommend you for sentencing!" With an
impulsive thrust of his gavel, he gestured for guards to
remove the prisoner.

Samuel was fully prepared for the death sentence, but
he was not immediately sentenced.

During the next five months, Samuel was summoned to

the court many times. He rarely heard anything new, only the same demeaning and confusing accusations. Yet, as wind strengthens the roots of a tree, so each session bolstered Samuel's confidence and deepened his sense of peace.

He heard the same diatribe over and over, month after month. His grandfather had worked in America. He himself cooperated with subversive missionaries who had been part of a scheme to destroy Chinese culture and enslave Chinese people. The religious school he attended in Wuzhou was known to be funded and supervised by the American CIA. His congregation had not cooperated with the approved organization. His sermons contradicted the scientific truths that at last were liberating China from centuries of superstition.

The government and Three-Self had found no hard evidence against him, no specifics. Thus, having lost face, they were forced to contrive justification for his arrest, or perhaps hoped he would confess so that they could use him as a valuable propaganda ploy.

One afternoon a guard came to Samuel's cell. "Parcel for Lamb," he said. The package from 35 Da Ma Zhan contained fried rice the way Sui Ling so deftly prepared it, cakes from his mother's recipes, two cans of meat, and a selection of fruit.

It was pleasant respite from prison fare. He shared the food with others in the prison. "You give to us?" one asked in surprise, a touch of suspicion in his voice.

"Flavor always improves when food is shared with friends," Samuel said, quoting an old proverb.

The delicacies raised new hope in the imprisoned pastor's heart. If his wife could send food, perhaps she could also come in person.

Not long afterward she did come. "I have tried and tried to come," Sui Ling told him, touching her eyes with the tip of a kerchief. "So have your mother and your sisters. At last, a kind police officer advised me how to send food and how to come see you. He was so helpful, it encouraged me to bring you a Bible."

Samuel held out his hands, anticipating. Sadly, his wife added, "The guards took it from me." Samuel withdrew his hands and became silent.

In those moments he gave thanks—as he had so often done—for this dearest of all people to him. She was slight and soft-spoken, with a reserved affection devoid of any aggression. Yet she was fully his, responsive to his love, eager to be alone with him. Now, however, unable to take her into his arms or so much as touch her, he found Sui Ling more fulfilling than he had ever known her to be, more even than on their wedding night.

She assured him of the family's good health and the health of close friends. "Have others of our people been taken?" Samuel asked. Sui Ling nodded.

The surveillance guard cleared his throat. Both knew they must speak carefully of such matters.

"The children miss you very much," Sui Ling said. She hesitated, taking firmer grip on her emotions. "They pray for you several times each day."

"The congregation?"

"We meet. People take an hour and more to assemble. We sing and pray softly." She smiled and added, "We are grateful for stormy nights with heavy rain."

"Greet them all. Tell them not to lose courage. Tell them God gives me peace and assurance."

Again the guard cleared his throat. "Visit finished," he said.

Samuel's beloved was escorted from him. She lingered at the exit door to lock her eyes in vicarious embrace with his. Then she was gone. As he was led like an animal back to his cell, it was almost as if she had not come.

Except for such limited family visits, providing scant information at most, Samuel knew little of the congregation at 35 Da Ma Zhan. He did not know that several of them paid a heavy price for their Christian faith. For instance, the Da Ma Zhan barber Yao Wei, a non-intellectual, was above political suspicion. But as a member of Pastor's Lamb's congregation, Yao Wei was not beyond potential use as a witness for the prosecution.

An emissary approached Yao Wei at his streetside business site. "You have an opportunity to serve your country," Yao Wei was told. "You will appear in court to testify against Samuel Lamb."

"But I—" the barber began to protest. The visitor raised his hand for silence.

"You will tell the court Mr. Lamb never speaks subversively in his public sermons. They are camouflage for his primary objectives. He secretly trains a small group to commit acts of sabotage in Guangzhou. You will tell the court that you refuse to participate in such a group."

"I can't say that!"

"If you value your freedom, you can!"

"But it would be lying. Also, Pastor Lamb is my friend. And most important, I am a Christian and can't speak falsely against anyone, especially against another believer!"

Yao Wei did not cut hair the next day. Or the next.

Yao Wei, too, was placed in a cell at Guangzhou Prison, his guilt clearly documented. He had blatantly demonstrated lack of patriotism. He must be appropriately punished.

When Samuel Lamb had entered prison, he had been permitted to take a Greek and English dictionary. He spent many hours reviewing words prominent in the New Testament.

Pistis—faith

Pistos—faithful

Eleos—mercy, merciful

Krisis—judgment

The dictionary provided a way for Samuel to minister to his cellmates. He could not overtly declare his faith. He could, however, respond to their questions. But he saw no visible signs of growth in them.

"A man from my *danwei* died," one of the men grumbled, speaking of his place of work. "At the funeral, an old man prayed a Christian prayer. Before he finished, the police took him. He got himself sentenced to eight years for public propaganda opposed to the government."

"So," said the second man to Samuel, "it is best we talk no more. Look where being a Christian put you!"

The mention of the *danwei* led Samuel to reflective thought. For the average Chinese, the *danwei* functioned as the primary source of identity and authority. The *danwei* may have been a factory, the neighborhood, a school, or some other unit to which the person submitted.

Samuel's *danwei* was the Three-Self organization, according to the officials and law officers who held him hostage. The realization gave him much distress. From the warmth of his heart he did not wish conflict with any person who claimed the Savior's name.

A person did not go to prison because a computer in Beijing produced a list of culprits: Accusation came from a person's *danwei*. The thought troubled Samuel deeply.

As everyone knew, a *danwei* might summon police intervention not only because a member had done wrong but also because the *danwei* wanted to rid itself of a hindrance to its own intentions. But if Three-Self had collaborated in Samuel's imprisonment, then why had he been urged to affiliate at the China Christian Council? He angished at the memory of what he had done, his willingness then to accept identity with Three-Self, his success in persuading his reluctant staff to comply.

His preaching had not changed after the council meetings. If anything, he had become bolder, preaching messages based on Ezekiel and Daniel, for example.

These thoughts persisted until one day, as Samuel stood before the judge, he heard the words: "This court sentences you to twenty years hard labor and the loss of all political rights for five years thereafter."

Although Samuel was grateful to have escaped the death sentence, he made an appeal. But the court refused to hear his protest. When his wife visited him, she asked wisely, "What is there to appeal for? You have not been given a just trial because the court had already made its decision beforehand."

The court voiced one note of leniency. Samuel's five-month incarceration leading up to the sentence would be deducted from the twenty-year sentence.

Danwei!

The word lingered in Samuel's thoughts as he set out on January 24, 1959, with a score of other prisoners on a journey across the country toward a labor camp, a livestock and tea plantation outside Shao Guan. For several days the convicts sat on the floor of an open truck as it jostled at brisk speed over the bumpy roads. People thronged the byways, pausing to gawk when someone called out "Prisoners!" Children laughed and pointed.

The men spoke quietly at first, testing the overseeing guard. But finding the guard less austere than some, the prisoners ventured more open conversation.

"They are taking us to be shot," said one man.

"I was held two years," said another. "I wish I had been put away in the first place."

"Why were you arrested?"

"The cadre over my *danwei* didn't like me."

"Did everyone else in your *danwei* dislike you as well?" the man was asked, and a strained wave of laughter briefly touched the group. They chattered more, voicing their fears, bemoaning their lot.

Hoping the noise of the truck and the chattering of the other prisoners would drown out the sound, Samuel sang quietly.

> *O what peace we often forfeit,*
> *O what needless pain we bear,*
> *All because we do not carry*
> *Everything to God in prayer.*

About to begin another stanza, he realized the men had stopped talking and were all listening to him. "What is your song?" a gruff voice asked.

Samuel smiled in quiet response.

"You are a Christian," another said.

"Don't you know?" said another. "He's the famous preacher we have read about in the newspapers!"

"O yes! Lamb! You are Pastor Lamb!"

"Labor camp will take the preaching out of him," said the guard. He spoke with levity, and the prisoners pleased him by laughing.

It was an introductory event for Samuel, preparing him for the many years in which witness would never happen easily. Yet, in that moment he promised God anew to give himself faithfully to every opportunity, however limited.

When the haggard group reached Shao Guan labor camp, there was enough daylight for Samuel to make a quick visual assessment. The central grounds consisted of a high-fenced enclosure with many guard stations that overlooked the whole area. Adjoining tea and tobacco fields flanked the prison area. A large herd of squealing hogs called out for their food; the stench of their pens reminded Samuel of the prison cell he had occupied in Guangzhou.

For Samuel's slight frame and limited energy, work became torture from the first morning. He was assigned to a clearance detail, grubbing out and burning old tea shrub to prepare for new seedlings. Working with shovel, pick, and axe, he became exhausted after only a few hours of work.

"You can do better than that!" a cadre criticized.

"They that wait upon the LORD shall renew their strength." Samuel laid desperate claim to the promise, and somehow he held up until sundown. He was incredulous when the cadre announced that since the day's quota of old stock had not been cleared away, the prisoners would work into the night.

Finally, when Pastor Lamb was like a blind man digging and chopping, the prisoners were told to lay down their tools and go for supper. Samuel had little appetite, but he knew he needed food for strength, so he forced down the cabbage gruel. He yearned for bed, but after a bell announced the end of the meal, he marched with the others to a lone structure off to one side of the complex. In it, guards herded prisoners into a stark lecture room, which had plain benches with no backs, barren walls except for a cracked blackboard.

After the group had been sitting twenty minutes, Samuel began to doze. "Wake up, you!" Someone from the row behind Samuel shoved a cruel fist into his ribs. "You'll put us all in trouble, and today will seem like it was an outing!"

Shortly after that, a teaching cadre appeared and stepped to the front. He gave the raised hand with closed fist salute. Most of the prisoners returned the gesture.

Samuel Lamb did not.

The cadre took no special note of compliance or resistance. He began, quoting one of the writings, "'Having made mistakes, you may feel that, come what may, you are saddled with them. If you have not made mistakes, you may feel that you are free from error and so become conceited.' My task in these next weeks, and the task of my compatriots who shall also face you, is to correct the mistakes of wrongdoers among us and destroy the pride of any or all.

"Your benevolent government has been forced to imprison you. Each of you is aware of his own guilt. But, mercifully, your government wishes to help you correct your bad thinking. Better an enlightened citizen than merely to inflict punishment."

He then spoke of the many wrongs in Chinese thinking. The people were like fields left unattended, he said. Now, mercifully, truth had come. "In the words of our beloved chairman," continued the lecturer, "'China has stood up!'" Bad thinking would be abolished from within and without.

The drudgery of each day's work became more unbearable for Samuel. Weariness seemed to infect his bones, and every day he faced the indoctrination classes, a wearying emotional tax on his body.

If cadres were displeased with progress in the fields, they kept the prisoners working long past sundown. But however long the workday, supper was always followed by a minimum of two hours in the lecture hall. Prisoners were required to study politics, evolution, and atheism. The nightly lectures consistently discredited Buddhism, denounced Islam, and spoke with disdain against Christianity.

"Are any of you Christians?" a cadre asked one evening. Samuel promptly nodded his head. The lecturer strode forward until he stood towering over his bold student. "Tell me," he said, his words crisp and calculated, "what has been the effect of Christianity on the world?"

Samuel kept silent. His heart cried heavenward for guidance.

"Give your answer!"

"Many people," came the cautious response, "have claimed to be Christians. Only a few have accepted the heart of the Christian message."

A smile touched the cadre's lips, grew, and broadened until he appeared to be quite pleased with what he was hearing. "So, then," the man assessed, "you agree that Christianity is a failure. In China it became the means whereby Americans and Europeans camouflaged their primary motives. Do you agree?"

Samuel remained silent. The cadre paused a moment. Then, impulsively, he grabbed Samuel's copy of the *Sayings*, found a passage and pointed to it. "Read these words!"

Samuel looked dutifully at the designated portion.

"Read it! Read aloud!"

"'Once the correct ideas characteristic of the advanced class are grasped by the masses,'" Samuel read, "'these ideas turn into a material force that changes society and changes the world.'"

"Splendid! Splendid!" exclaimed the cadre. "You are making early and fruitful progress!" He snatched the book, holding it high. "What is it the Christians say? Hallelujah! Ah, yes, that's it!" He turned again to Samuel. "You see, I once sat at the feet of white-bellied missionaries. They lived in their fine mansions, in their high-walled seclusions, and told our poverty-stricken people to believe in God. 'Be rich in your hearts,' they said, 'while we grow rich in our pockets!'"

A Catholic priest also sat in the study group, and the cadre also singled him out for special note and attention.

Prisoners had only occasional opportunity for personal conversation, but Samuel and the priest were assigned to work in one partially secluded area, and occasionally they found themselves alone together.

"We will be asked to denounce our faith," the priest said fearfully. "What will you do?"

"My faith is my life," Samuel told him. "I could never deny it."

"You are a Protestant clergyman?"

"I am a lay preacher."

"But you seem so sure of what you believe."

"As the apostle Paul wrote to Timothy, 'I know whom I have believed, and am convinced that he is able to guard what I have entrusted to him.'"

"You have committed much of the Bible to memory?"

"Not as much as I wish I had done."

A guard walked nearby. Samuel and the priest busied themselves.

When they were once more alone, the priest said, "I had memorized much of the prayer book. At times, however, when fear takes full hold on me, I remember scarcely any of it. One morning, after I had had a frightening dream, I could hardly quote the rosary."

"Perhaps," Samuel ventured cautiously, "you have come to a time when the formalities of your religion have little meaning to you, a time when you need to flee to Christ alone."

Tears came to the priest's eyes. Samuel prayed for guidance. *Always be prepared to give an answer,* he remembered from 1 Peter 3, *to everyone who asks you to give the reason for the hope that you have.*

But the priest did not ask. He only looked at Samuel in agony of spirit.

"I will pray for you," Samuel said. The two had no further confrontations.

A few weeks later the cadre called both of them to the front of the lecture hall. "You will demonstrate for us," he said. "You will show the others an example of good progress in adhering to the admonitions of our great leader." He then called on the priest to renounce his faith openly.

The priest complied.

He slandered the pope. He denounced Mary and declared the Virgin Birth a myth. He castigated the Roman Catholic Church as a capitalist monster stealing from the poor to make its prelates rich. He very nearly collapsed from the agony of the ordeal.

Samuel looked on in pity. Then his turn came. He

remembered the promise from James, *If any of you lacks wisdom, he should ask God, who gives generously to all.*

Other cadres, having been told what would happen that night, also sat at the front. They leaned forward, awaiting the words of the well-known *muk si* from Guangzhou.

"Christianity has been made a mockery by those so-called Christians who question the teachings of the Bible," Samuel began. "They deny the inspiration of the Scriptures. They speak of the miracles performed by Jesus as myths. They also classify much of the Old Testament events as merely traditions." Samuel noticed the cadres. They listened intently, their faces expressing pleasure at what they heard.

So Samuel continued, eloquently denouncing liberalism and shallow Christianity. He derided syncretism, fanaticism, hypocrisy, gossip, covetousness, backsliding, secularism in the church, materialism in the lives of Christians, spiritual pride, complacency, and disobedience.

The cadres were elated.

That night Samuel Lamb lay quietly on his bed. Outside, the night hovered somber and still. A light breeze moved imperceptibly, carrying with it the pig-yard stench, which wafted into the dormitory.

Years of incarceration lay ahead of Guangzhou's demeaned pastor. He might be in prison until he died. Yet, in this quiet moment Samuel Lamb felt like a free man, emancipated by the tender of promises beyond the scope of prison bars. "If any of you lacks wisdom . . ."

In the depths of his heart Samuel was a man at peace. He knew the Shepherd who had led him this night would lead him through whatever the future might hold.

"If any of you lacks wisdom . . ."

Hallelujah!

9

SAMUEL LAMB BECAME PAINFULLY AWARE that imprisonment for known guilt would be more acceptable than facing two decades of incarceration with neither judge's nor jury's conviction of any crime. He did not have democracy's option of appeal, no attorney to advocate for him, no redress. In his humanness, he might have complained.

But he didn't.

Samuel Lamb was totally helpless, which drove him to complete dependence on the Lord. He could do nothing for his family but entrust them wholly to the Father's care. He had no way to earn any money. His very breath was a pawn in the hands of others. And yet he was at peace. Hallelujah!

And the Presence? While never visible, the Presence walked beside him as a constant reality, assuring him: "Peace I leave with you; my peace I give you. I do not give to you as the world gives. Do not let your hearts be troubled and do not be afraid."

Yet Samuel sensed a dissatisfaction. Although he did not ask for material possessions or for assurances of personal safety and ultimate freedom, in the heart of his heart he longed for a Bible. If only he could hold in his hands a copy of God's Word and drink in the verses of the Eternal Message. If only . . .

But he did have the Bible—hidden in his heart.

During the tedious hours at work and the long hours on his insect-infested bed, Samuel drew from the Scripture verses he had memorized.

He found the prison Epistles especially rich. "What has happened to me has really served to advance the gospel," Paul had written to his compatriots in Philippi. Samuel Lamb wondered how those verses could apply to his case.

At times he seemed to be looking down a long tunnel, an endless cavity of dense and mocking darkness. He saw himself a prisoner until he died. Only a fool would harbor hope of having his sentence commuted. Pardon was equally inconceivable. More likely, the officials would add years to his sentence, with little or no justification.

So how could his circumstances serve to advance the Gospel? Would he find a parish of opportunity here?

He witnessed faithfully, ever responsive to the smallest window of opportunity, quietly singing at work, identifying himself as a Christian whenever he could. Labor camp provided opportunities for closer associations than had Guangzhou Prison. Even so, guards kept close surveillance, not only imprisoning his body but also attempting to imprison his mind and lips as well.

Samuel thought about the words Paul had written to the beleaguered Christians at Rome: *If we live, we live to the Lord; and if we die, we die to the Lord. So, whether we live or die, we belong to the Lord.* In the year 1959, Samuel Lamb 'lived.

Into the winter months Samuel minded pig barns, lugged food to animals, and carried provisions to the warehouses— tasks his slight frame could manage. With the coming of spring, however, his situation worsened. He was transferred again to a crew clearing land for additional crops. He liked being outdoors, but the work involved long hours and hard labor. The Presence spoke comforting words to him: "Your strength will equal your days," echoing Moses' final words of blessing on Israel.

Prisoners received one day off every two weeks. Mornings of such days were designated for personal laundry and cleaning the barracks. Bed bugs thrived, but when prisoners asked if they could take their cots and blankets out into the sun and scrub their sleeping quarters with lye solution, the cadres only laughed. "This is a prison, not a hotel!" they reminded the prisoners. "When you scratch your welts, remind yourselves how fortunate you are to be alive and how you could be free and privileged like us if you had heeded the wise counsels of our beloved chairman!"

One spring mail call, Samuel received a letter from his sister Ai Ling, who announced she would try to visit him on a certain day. When the day came, Samuel gathered a small bundle of unneeded clothing to send back for use by someone else and took it with him to his day's assignment—to the consternation of his group leader, somewhat paranoid by nature, who accused him of contemplating escape.

His sister did come, with several items for her brother. "Mother is concerned about your health," she said, producing a thermos, "and sent you some tonic soup." The group leader told Samuel he could not drink the soup because it probably contained poison. At the indoctrination session that night, one of the cadres reported an attempted escape and a thwarted suicide. Samuel could only shake his head.

One morning the cadre supervising Samuel's detail showed him a large plot of land. "You will clear away all the brush—down to the roots, not just cut off at the top." For a crew of men, the assignment would be formidable enough. For hands more adept at playing piano keys than handling a spade and axe, the job appeared insurmountable.

Believing it his Christian duty and privilege to perform assignments capably, Samuel tackled the area with full energy. By noon, however, the land showed little evidence of his efforts. Only a small cart half-filled with grubbed-out brush documented his labor. Weariness penetrated to his bone marrow. He repeatedly reminded himself, *I can do all things through Christ which strengtheneth me.*

The cadre came, stood a long moment with his hands on his hips, and surveyed the area. "You work too slow," he said. "Liven up, or I will be expected to report you for disciplinary duty." Disciplinary duty had taken the lives of some men.

Samuel wanted the supervisor to see the cart. He knew the man was impatient and touchy, however, and kept silent. *Please, Lord*, he prayed in his heart, *make him see what work I have done.*

The cadre swaggered away. Then, for no apparent reason, he turned and came directly alongside the cart. There he paused, looked out toward Samuel, into the cart, and out toward Samuel once more.

"You!" the man cried out. "Did you grub the roots in this cart?"

"I did, sir."

"You alone?"

"Yes, sir."

Samuel supposed he detected a hint of admiration on the man's face. Cautiously, because he was so very tired, Samuel sat on the cart's edge for a minute, expecting the cadre to order him to his feet.

The cadre said nothing and walked away. A few minutes later, Samuel summoned the energy to get to his feet and continue. The Presence whispered to him: "They that wait upon the LORD shall renew their strength." Samuel knew it was true.

This plot of land became to Samuel Lamb a visual parable of China's church in which the Holy Spirit permitted suffering as preparation for seedtime and harvest. Was also it a parable of his own plight and his own future? He thought about promises from the Psalms: *Weeping may remain for a night, but rejoicing comes in the morning.*

Would there be morning? Or would Samuel Lamb's life and service end in this labor camp?

One day, refreshed from a long night's sleep, he progressed beyond the halfway point on his land-clearing assignment. With high spirits he sang:

> *I live for Him, who died for me.*
> *In sufferings sore, His grace I see.*

His loving kindness calms my soul
Though angry billows o'er me roll.

He became aware of someone alongside him. "I listen to your song and the words," a fellow prisoner said. "Is it one of the gods about which you sing?"

"It is the Lord Jesus," Samuel said.

The man did not understand.

"My body is in bondage, just as yours is," Samuel continued. "But my soul has been set free by the grace of the true and only God." The identity of Jesus the Savior, the merit of his mercy, and the unleashing of his power in his death and resurrection were as new to this man as the contrasting teachings he heard each night at indoctrination sessions.

"I've watched you many days," he said. "At first I thought you were a fool, thinking the dragon's teeth to be stones with which children play. But a light shines from within you."

Two weeks later the man became Samuel's Christian brother.

There were others. New believers emerged out of the darkness of the prison like brands snatched from the burning.

Samuel knew that in the Lord's sovereignty, he had the right to permit imprisonment so that the gospel message could be shared with those who hungered but had no other table at which to eat. How utterly beyond counting—the worth of a person's soul!

Nightly indoctrination sessions taxed Samuel's energy as much as the work of each preceding day. It was not that he in any way doubted. In fact, the nightly tirades bolstered his convictions. But he grew soul-weary from the continual onslaughts of false teachings and the assumption—indeed, the requirement—that he should embrace the evil beliefs.

"China fell prey to twin opiums," one of the teaching cadres liked to repeat. "There was the stupefying dust carried on those British ships and the missionaries who journeyed with the foul cargo. How discerning was the great Lenin, when he said, 'Religion is the opiate of the people'!"

One night the cadre attacked Buddhism. "Have you read the writings of Lord Buddha concerning how confused even he became with the teachings of the Blessed One? 'The world is finite, the world is infinite; the soul and the body are identical,' and with the next stroke of the brush, it is said, 'The soul is one thing, the body another; the saint exists after death, the saint does not exist after death.'"

Another night he lashed out, "You foolish Muslims. You hate the Christians. You fight the Israelis. Do you read the Koran? The prophet places Christians, Jews, and Muslims as equals. The sacred books of each, according to Muhammad and the Koran, point the way to heaven."

Then came the night when, following an impassioned lecture on China's new thinking as the crowning apex of physical and social evolution, the cadre said, "Christianity must no longer be permitted to delay the destiny of our beloved country. Your government is patient. Penalties must be regretfully inflicted on some persistent zealots who cannot or will not be rid of their blindness. But your government also knows the death knell for Christianity has sounded. Christianity is not simply dying in China. Christianity is already dead and in rigor mortis!"

He paused, apparently awed by his own eloquence. "Prisoner Lamb," he resumed bluntly, "do you enjoy continuing progress in your rejection of Christianity, as you so ably informed us several months ago?"

Samuel's heart sank. He hoped by now the cadre would have forgotten the incident. He hesitated a long and distressing moment.

"Your delay consumes time to which you have no right!" the cadre snapped.

"Christianity is a broad term," Samuel said cautiously. "The genuine Christian experiences life in Christ rather than membership in a religion. Only in that sense can it be said he is involved in what is commonly called Christianity."

The cadre stared at him for several moments, then dismissed the session.

"Do you want a bullet in the back of your head?" one of the inmates asked as the men prepared to sleep.

"And in the back of some of ours for good measure!" snapped another.

Samuel smiled, not otherwise responding. Actually, the incident broadened Samuel's influence among many of the prisoners.

As the first year passed, his faith become more widely known. Witness opportunities increased, but always under the most cautious circumstances, always with discernment. He knew he dare not take the initiative but must wait for someone to approach him, to make the first move. He also knew he might be approached by someone pretending spiritual interest only to spy on him.

Even in his best times Samuel had only a few opportunities for evangelism. He could number on his fingers those who professed belief, and of those who did, several turned back.

"You are inviting the bullet," warned one inmate.

"I would rather live and go to hell," quipped another, "than die and go to heaven!"

Not only did Samuel sense the responsibility of faithful outreach, but he also knew the importance of discipling. In the meal lineup, he might stand near enough a new believer to whisper, "Keep in your mind these days a Scripture verse that says, 'I can do all things through Christ.' Just those words. Repeat them over and over. When problems arise, quietly remind the Lord of his promise and see how surely he does provide!"

As the men assembled for nightly indoctrination, the anguished countenance of another would prompt Samuel to say, "Draw nigh to God and he will draw nigh to you." Sometimes he would find a new believer writing a letter, and dictate for him a promise to mull over in future meditation, like Paul's words to the Philippians, "Do not be anxious about anything, but in everything, by prayer and petition, with thanksgiving, present your requests to God. And the peace of God, which transcends all understanding, will guard your hearts and your minds in Christ Jesus."

If only I could convene a Bible study for these fledgling believers, he thought. How wonderful it would be, providing them all with paper and pencil as he quoted God's Word, helping them understand it, and answering their questions.

As the months slowly passed, however, his ability to remember Scripture verses faded. He had memory lapses and had to work very hard to recall references to certain ideas.

Often at night, resisting sleep, he silently quoted chapters, sometimes even entire epistles. Except for the Psalms, he had memorized only New Testament books and portions. It occurred to him that he was neglecting the Old Testament. Did he even remember the order of the books? In desperation one night, like a boy in Sunday school, he reviewed the list of books of the Bible. "Genesis, Exodus, Leviticus, Numbers, Deuteronomy," he intoned softly, "Joshua, Judges, Ruth . . ."

He lingered there—thinking of Sui Ling. Months had passed without so much as a letter from her. "All mail goes through the commandant's office," one prisoner had said. "Who knows what happens to it from there?"

Samuel continued the list, coming to the minor prophets. "Hosea, Joel, Amos, Obadiah . . ."

Obadiah? Samuel Lamb could not so much as recall the content of the book.

"Hosea writes of Israel's apostasy," he said quietly, as if teaching himself. "And Joel . . . ah, yes, LORD. In Joel you said, 'I will pour out my Spirit on all people.' Is this for China, even in perilous times such as these?"

He continued his review. "Amos—Israel's restoration and the glory of David's kingdom." He had often preached from Amos. But Obadiah?

"O God!" he prayed aloud. "If only I had a Bible!"

"Quiet back there!" the floor monitor reprimanded from the dormitory's far end.

In silence Samuel continued stretching his memory. Obadiah?

Anguishing guilt taunted him. How dare he permit any content of God's Word to slip so totally from his recollection?

Then, gloriously, he remembered a text he had once selected from Obadiah! How did it go? "As you have done . . ."

Yes! Yes! Now he had it, the whole of the text! "The day of the Lord is near for all nations. As you have done, it will be done to you; your deeds will return upon your own head."

Obadiah!

The living Word of the living God, promising to bless his witness. Samuel Lamb—in this place a nonentity, in God's sight a chosen and worthy vessel of service.

Hallelujah!

10

ONE OF THE PERIPHERAL BLESSINGS that made Shao Guan labor camp tolerable was its rural setting. In springtime—when bud and blossom, leaf and stalk, reflected the Creator's handiwork—Samuel looked on in awe and reverence.

How had Solomon expressed it? "See! The winter is past . . . flowers appear on the earth . . . the cooing of doves is heard in our land."

Samuel could remember only a portion, possibly more, if he had tried. But the text was from Song of Songs, and it turned his mind back to thoughts of Sui Ling. How he missed her strength and tenderness, her individuality and rapport, her totalness. It was a distraction the Good Shepherd must surely condone.

Even the joy of spring and recollections of his wife, however, could not assuage the continuing torment of field labor. Further complicating his distress, Samuel was reassigned to a tobacco field. Because he was a separationist by theology and an advocate of clean lifestyle, he chafed at the prospect. "Lord," he prayed, "it is not mine to choose. You know how I abhor tobacco. I can only trust that you have permitted this change in my activities. I will take it for your glory."

The tobacco field had been turned by oxen and plow. Samuel was instructed to draw the loose topsoil into ridges, using a primitive hoe. It was taxing work. Although he found the newly tilled earth light and yielding, thrusting the hoe and drawing dirt into a high field-length ridge soon activated the pain and weariness in his slender arms.

In the middle of the morning the imperious overseer inspected Samuel's effort. "Your ridge is not straight!" he barked. Others paused to watch the scene, giving the cadre an audience. "Have you ever done agricultural work before?"

"I have not, sir."

"Filthy rich," the cadre muttered. "Probably didn't look after your own clothes until you came here." He looked at Samuel's crooked ridge. "You build a row straight by drawing a line."

"A line?" Samuel asked. "Do I make a mark on the ground?"

"No, idiot!" Nearby observers laughed. "A line is a string!" the cadre scoffed. "A string, understand?"

"I do not have a string, sir."

"Then get one. From the commissary. Before you go, finish leveling this row so you can measure correctly."

"The entire row, sir?" Samuel asked. Laughter echoed in his ears.

The cadre swaggered on, and Samuel began his task. His hands had softened since he had cleared rock and brush in the tea field. They now began to blister before he had finished leveling even the first half of the tobacco row. He plucked some large leaves on a nearby tree and used them to pad his hands against the hoe.

When the leaves tore and disintegrated into pieces, Samuel went for a fresh supply, but the cadre called out, forbidding him. "Be careful!" the cadre added. "This is government property. It's against regulations to strip leaves from trees!"

"Government property?" muttered a man nearby. "It's private property confiscated from the rightful owners."

"It would appear," responded another, "that prison standards are a change from your accustomed comforts and conveniences." Laughter once more.

At last Samuel was able to level the soil once again. Then he went to the commissary to get some string. The inmate at the dispensing counter drawled, "String? Give me your requisition, comrade."

"I need string for field measurement," Samuel said.

"I did not ask what you need it for, did I? I said to give me your requisition." He folded his arms. "If I dispense string to fly kites, we both will get disciplined. I lose my easy job, and you go into solitary or worse. Now you wouldn't want that to happen, would you? Would you, friend? Not to me or to you. Oh, no!"

Samuel loathed such arrogance, but held his poise.

The man looked around and smirked as he said, "Did you hear why the commandant doesn't allow prostitutes at Shao Guan? It's because—"

"Where do I secure a requisition?" Samuel interrupted.

The inmate, having been affronted in his stand-up comedy performance, glared a moment and said, "You get requisitions from your cadre, stupid!"

"My cadre was the one who sent me." This caught the inmate off guard. "I will go to him," Samuel said, turning away.

"Wait!" the inmate called out, his voice suddenly amiable. "Where do you work? In the fields?"

"In the tobacco field," said Samuel.

The inmate whistled. "Even the Devil runs when he sees your superior!" He glanced about cautiously. "I've been at Shao Guan for five years, and he's the worst I've been shouted at by. He came storming in here one day—"

"May I have the string?" Samuel interrupted.

"Of course! Of course! If your cadre is keeping a clock on you, a man doesn't want to dally, does he? I've heard the commandant say your cadre is a paper man with the mouth of a tiger and the heart of a mouse. But then the commandant can say what he wills of whomever, can't he? If the commandant says you die at dawn, you die at dawn, don't you? There's those of whom he has said just that, be sure! May it never be one of us two, eh? Never one of us!"

"My string, please!"

"In my own case, me having watched cadres come and go for five years, and of them all I stay farthest from yours. Like I started to say before, he came at me here one morning—"

"Please, friend, my string! Must I go for the requisition?"

"No need! No need! Honest faces come from honest hearts, as one wiser than I long ago said."

Finally the prison clerk turned to walk back to the store shelves and returned with a ball of string. "Sign this release for me."

When Samuel reached the door, the man added, "Got time for me to tell you why the commandant doesn't allow—"

Samuel walked quickly on and did not hear the rest of the clerk's story. When he returned to the field, Samuel's cadre was engaged in a scathing tirade against some other prisoner's ineptness, so Samuel went quietly to work. After he had restructured the planting row, straight as the flight of a migrant bird, his cadre scrutinized his work and apparently approved, because he sent him for fertilizer.

"Fertilizer?" Samuel asked.

"Honey buckets. Up by the cesspools."

As a boy in Macau and during the years in Hong Kong and Wuzhou, Samuel had seen honey buckets, containers of human waste, dangling from shoulder yokes borne by laborers. It had never occurred to him, however, that he might one day have to carry something so wretched. During early spring, rebellious inmates filled out their punishment by emptying cesspools and filling verminous containers with the winter's excrement. These containers, these honey buckets, stood in profusion alongside the cistern-like openings to the underground pits.

Samuel selected a yoke from a stack and bent down to fasten a bucket to one end. The stench wafted upward to his nostrils, gagging him for a moment and driving him a step backward. "O Lord," he mumbled, "only by your grace can I endure this!"

Holding his breath, he fastened buckets to each end of the yoke and stooped to shoulder the harness. As he tried to stand, his strength faltered, and the weight of the buckets pulled him downward. He took a deep, sustaining breath and caught the full aroma of the stench. It was like anesthesia, causing him to push the yoke from him, almost tipping over the buckets.

"Careful!" a voice called. "That's prison gold. Spill a drop and they make you eat the rest!"

Samuel did not look to identify inmate or cadre. He shouldered the yoke a second time, lifted it, and managed faltering steps toward the tobacco field, but again put down the load, his shoulders aching. "I cannot, Lord! I cannot!" He remembered a promise from a psalm: *The eyes of the LORD are on the righteous and his ears are attentive to their cry.* He clung to the promise and prayed aloud, "Hear my cry, O Lord! Help me!"

Again he put his shoulder to the yoke, again looked out at the distant field, again put down the load. He could not possibly carry so much so far. There remained no alternative. Leaving the yoke and one bucket behind, he picked up the second container. It took all his strength just to carry one bucket.

Shifting the load from his right hand to his left, from his left hand to his right, he struggled forward. Even so, his arms felt half-drawn from their sockets. His heart pounded at a frenzied pulse. He gasped for breath, each time drawing the pungent stench into his tormented lungs. "O Lord!" he called out, again and again. Once he all but stumbled and fell, which would have spilled murk onto himself and into the path.

"You!" the cadre shouted, as Samuel put down the bucket to rest at the edge of the field. "Procedure is to come with two, not one!"

How did a man five-and-a-half-feet tall, weighing scarcely a hundred pounds, manage such a demand? "I am sorry, sir!" Samuel called out. He heard a chorus of laughter.

Once at the tobacco row, he rested as long as he dared, then set to the task. With one hand he dug pits in the soil. With the other hand he dipped into the bucket and brought up gluts of feculence, which he dropped into each hole. To a man of such gentle spirit, to hands familiar with Beethoven and Mozart, it was utter horror.

"O God!" he gasped aloud. The sight and the smell wrenched his stomach until he vomited.

The cadre stood watching, laughing. "Good work! Good work! Dip your puke into the seed holes, too! I will see to it you earn merit for your resourcefulness!"

Again Samuel heard the laughter. The others laughed partly over Samuel's plight, but primarily in deference to the cadre.

Samuel felt the first pangs of self-pity, but then from the former inmate of another prison came the words: "I count all things but loss for the excellency of the knowledge of Christ Jesus my Lord . . . and do count them but dung. . . . I have learned, in whatsoever state I am, therewith to be content. I know both how to be abased, and I know how to abound. . . . I can do all things through Christ which strengtheneth me."

Like a cool wind, like a cleansing downfall of rain came the undergirding, empowering Word of God. Samuel returned to work, and once again his heart was at peace. When time came to fetch additional fertilizer, he again attempted to lug two honey buckets instead of one, but he fared no better than before.

"Help me, Lord," he prayed. He labored his way down the path with one bucket.

"You!" The cadre was furious. "How is it you expect favor others are denied? Rewrite the regulations, would you?"

Samuel stood full height and looked the man in the eye. He was aware of the Presence. "I ask no favors, sir," he said quietly. "I have not the strength to do as much as others, but I will never shirk within the scope of my ability."

Rudely, the cadre pulled open Samuel's clothes. "Bones and skin but not much gristle, is there, comrade?"

Samuel lifted the hurt of the raucous laughter to the One

who said, "Cast thy burden upon the LORD, and He shall sustain thee."

The cadre shrugged his shoulders and went elsewhere. Samuel resumed work with a continued plea for strength.

"You shouldn't have talked back to him," a prisoner nearby said. "It could make things bad for all of us."

"They have ways to deal with people like you," said another. Samuel grew troubled at the thought of having acted unwisely.

Later that night, as prisoners formed lines to go into the indoctrination classes, an inmate slipped into the shadows beside Samuel. Like a ventriloquist, he spoke clearly but without moving his lips. "I saw you in the field today," he said. "I have watched you before and have spoken with others about you. I am told you are a believer in God. I want to talk to you."

"March!" a cadre called out.

As Samuel entered the lecture hall with the others, he prayed in silent gratitude. It had been the most difficult day of his life. In that moment of weariness and darkness he did not see how he could face another. Yet, as long as he was touching hearts in need of the Savior, he knew assuredly he was in the place where his Lord needed him to be. He knew the Lord would also give him strength.

The Presence whispered, "If the LORD delights in a man's way, he makes his steps firm."

Might it be ever so!

Pastor Samuel Lamb, 1989.

世界地图

Above: Pastor Lamb points to the area in Northern China, Shansi Province, where he spent fifteen years of forced labor in a coal mine.

Above Right: With American astronaut Jim Irwin, one of the many prominent visitors to the church. Irwin shows him a simulated moon rock.

Below Right: Evangelist Billy Graham featured Pastor Lamb and the congregation in a nationwide telecast.

Above Left: July 6, 1980. With participants in first new convert baptism.

Below Left: July 4, 1951. Lamb's wedding party.

Above: Pastor Lamb, himself a concert pianist, plays Mozart for visiting American musician Dino Kartsonakis.

Above Left: Typical worship group in the sanctuary at Guangzhou. Membership grew from four to more than a thousand in ten years.

Below Left: The pastor delivers a sermon. He speaks conversationally, and sermons rarely take less than an hour and forty-five minutes.

Above: The entrance to 35 Da Ma Zhan. More than a thousand people went in and out of this entrance every week.

Above: Beloved Zhu Feng buried booklets published by Pastor Lamb, sparing them from destruction by Red Guards during the so-called "Cultural Revolution."

Above Right: The church's tape-duplicating equipment, shown here, and all of its books, hymnals, and tracts, were confiscated in the February 1990 police raid.

Below Right: Weekly communion service

Above Left: One of the Three-Self churches in Guangzhou.

Below Left: Blind and fearless, Miss Youn is a retired school teacher who comes to the church every morning to pray for her pastor and the work.

Above: Pastor Lamb's study—a tiny cubicle behind the small platform. All of his books were taken by police during the February 1990 raid.

A typical service—wall-to-wall people.

Many people hear the Gospel for the first time.

Sunday school. The teacher was one of the church's first six converts.

The church "parking lot."

Lamb visits a young Christian family. Earlier Red Guards had dug four feet deep under the floor in search of illicit Bibles.

"Please tell us—what does it mean to be a Christian?"

A visiting acupuncture doctor from Northern China tells of severe persecution in his region.

Visitors from the north. Some Christians travel thousands of miles to discuss house church ministry with Pastor Lamb.

11

DAY AFTER DAY of tobacco planting left Samuel numb with weariness. Could a man die of exhaustion? Was his inability to work at the pace of others a hindrance to his witness? Could low productivity jeopardize a prisoner's status, even his life?

"Lord," he prayed one morning, that week of the torturous tobacco-field assignment, "I don't ask for an easy load. I only ask for a load I have enough strength to bear." Into his mind came another promise from the Psalms: *God is our refuge and strength, an ever-present help in trouble.*

Did he believe this? Could he praise God even in the midst of trouble, whatever the surrounding circumstances, however bleak the looming horizons? "Praise the Lord!" he called out against the wind sweeping toward him from the tobacco field. He was alone and no one overheard.

Had not Job affirmed, "Though he slay me, yet will I hope in him"?

Yes! Yes! Ever his name be praised!

That very day Samuel's cadre gave him a lighter assignment in the field. "You will deliver seedlings to the planters," he said. "That should not be beyond your meager strength."

Laughter came from a few men who overheard. Silent praise came from the heart of Samuel Lamb.

It was brisk work, as demanding as any of the field tasks, but Samuel had strength enough to do it. Others had been subjects of cadre tirades demanding brisker action. Not Samuel Lamb. He hustled through long days, never once leaving a row of workers unsupplied.

When he returned to camp at night, weariness came over him with a deadening pallor. He sat, stupefied at times, through after-supper indoctrination lectures.

During the long nights on his bed he repeatedly prayed, "O my Father, you promise strength for each day. Your children's strength is perfected in weakness. Give me deliverance, I plead!"

The Presence whispered back, "Do not be anxious about anything . . ."

Even in the bleakness of his situation, Samuel Lamb's faith increased.

One morning, when work crew calls were issued, Samuel's name did not appear on the tobacco-field roster. Had he been overlooked? But then the daily enumerator called out, "Now the weaklings." Laughter followed his announcement, as Samuel once again became the butt of scorn because he was listed from then on with those of limited capability.

He looked after the swine herd for a few days, enduring stench almost as revolting as that of the honey buckets, but the work was not as strenuous. If he ever again had opportunity to preach a sermon about the follies of the Prodigal Son . . .

One morning at job call he was asked to report to headquarters. As he walked apprehensively to the headquarters building, he wondered why he had been summoned. Would he be disciplined? The assuring voice of the Presence reminded him, "We know that in all things God works for the good of those who love him."

Chinese prison camps did not publish honor rolls. Inmates received no citations, no stroking, no pats on the back, no verbal commendations. To his delight, however, Samuel discovered he had been singled out as a convict of satisfactory conduct and performance. Even in the trauma of the tobacco field, his superior had apparently noted that he had extended himself to the fullest effort, made no complaints, and sincerely tried to comply.

Because Samuel had come into a measure of good favor, he was assigned clerical work, then supervisory roles such as overseeing others assigned to office functions. "Lord," he prayed, "if I once complained, forgive me. You are my Shepherd in both the major and minor situations of my life."

Media reports can be expected to accentuate the negative. Someone has said that anything ever heard about China is probably happening, at any given time, somewhere in China. But, as previously stated, China is a land of long traditions, and the traditions include intricate legalities. Nightly indoctrination sessions at Shao Guan Labor Camp, and scores of other labor camps, were held with the specific objective of producing men who adhered to, if not overtly supported, socialist dogma and programs.

Samuel, for example, developed with considerable skill (having two decades to polish such craft!) the ability to answer a lecturer's inquiry with "according to the book" or "as you have said" without thereby indicating either disbelief or acceptance.

Often alone on tasks with the men under him, Samuel had numerous opportunities for witness and occasional joys of harvest. He was grateful. Yet he longed to touch all of the prisoners, to pastor a non-preaching parish that would include every man at Shao Guan labor camp. He often prayed for that opportunity.

One morning the commandant himself summoned Samuel into his office. "Have you any experience as a barber?" he asked bluntly. Samuel was speechless. The commandant explained that the camp barber had completed his sentence, and no one had been found to take his place. The replacement needed to be someone who had basic tonsorial skills but also an established record of dependability and trustworthiness. Samuel Lamb left the commandant's office with new orders: He was the camp's new barber.

He remembered the words from 1 Corinthians: "There are different kinds of service . . . different kinds of working."

The new position seemed almost like a commuted sentence. Samuel marveled at how distinctly the Lord had led him—from those fellow students in Hong Kong and his village street shop to cutting the hair of his fellow inmates of Shao Guan.

His new superior watched him less than an hour, quickly assuring himself Samuel Lamb was, in fact, a barber. Samuel needed only to report for work at the beginning of the day. He enjoyed much freedom and could go about from place to place, set his own schedules, work at his own speed. Most of all, he met prisoners he would only see occasionally before but with whom he now could become acquainted and share his faith. The camp officials increasingly trusted Samuel, allowing him to go to places of limited security, even approving occasional journeys to nearby areas that were off-limits to other prisoners.

Samuel took his working kit to dormitories, hallways, and the clinic. He even went outside on warm days, selecting quiet nooks where he could speak freely with his customers. God had, indeed, given him a parish.

As he cut the men's hair, he asked them about their families and their past life. He never discussed the reasons that either of them had been incarcerated, and he immediately changed the subject if complaints arose or conversation turned toward politics. When he sensed a man was rebellious or discouraged, he tried to cheer the man with lighthearted joking. Whomever his customer or whatever the subject of their conversation, soul-winner Samuel Lamb kept ever alert for the opening of a "witness window."

"Lord," he prayed, "the apostle Paul says he planted the seed, and Apollos watered it, but he says you made it grow. Here, though, it seems I am the only one to plant and water. Show me how to proceed wisely so you can make the seed grow."

With customers sitting for repeat cuttings, it would

sometimes require several visits before Samuel found the window into which he could shine the light of the Gospel. Other men opened the window for him. "What wrong sent you here?" some would ask. Samuel always avoided answering that question. To say he knew no reason for his arrest would be to fall into the prison syndrome of claiming a bum rap. At times like these he would pray, awaiting the Holy Spirit's guidance. He knew that stool pigeons stalked like hunters, seeking trophies to lay before the commandant, hoping thereby to gain bounty on their own behalf.

Samuel often hummed the melody of a hymn as he worked, both as expression of the joy ever in his heart and as a signal to other believers. "You are a Christian," someone would say.

In this way he identified a family of believing friends. They could not gather for fellowship, but having identified themselves, they passed eye-glance greetings when they saw each other and gave nonverbal encouragement when they were forced to listen to atheistic teaching at the nightly lectures.

It discouraged Samuel to find so many believers reticent in witness, some out of cowardice, most unsure of how to proceed. "When we walk in the will of God," he told one shy young man, "we are ever in his watch. We become responsible for the opportunities given us at any moment, wherever we may be, no matter who hears us. We can always know the Lord is watching over us and the Holy Spirit is using us. Never forget my friend, we are God's fellow workers!"

"But it would be death to quote a Scripture verse to someone like the commandant," the young man said.

"Not unless our death was the Shepherd's only means of touching such a person. More likely, the Holy Spirit would find for us the opportune moment, the exact word to speak."

"You witness to many here?"

"As the Holy Spirit leads. The Holy Spirit is not a weapon in our hands. We are the tools in his."

Samuel's new responsibilities brought both believing and unbelieving people to his attention. They came to him—the weak, the wayward, the fearful, and the faithful, but he also attracted the suspicious. "I want to believe you are truly Christian," said one prisoner, as Samuel began cutting his hair, "but for an inmate to be as happy and optimistic as you seem to be, he must be cooperating with the cadres in some way."

"Cooperating or submitting?" Samuel asked.

"What do you mean?"

"You have read the book of Romans?"

"I read it so long ago I hardly remember any of it."

"In Romans 13," Samuel continued, "the apostle writes: 'Everyone must submit himself to the governing authorities, for there is no authority except that which God has established. The authorities that exist have been established by God.'"

"We must agree with those over us?"

"Not necessarily agree, but always obey."

"But what about the teachings, the atheism?"

"Do you remember the story of Daniel in the Old Testament? He obeyed the laws of Babylon. Yet when he was told not to pray, he boldly refused to submit."

"You know the whole Bible by heart?"

"By no means. I have not seen a Bible since we came to this camp. But many verses are in my memory. We Christians must search our minds even for fragments of Scripture and must hold every phrase of God's Word as a treasure—to sustain us personally and to share with others."

"I could perhaps quote John 3:16 and Psalm 23."

"You can bring many to Jesus and encourage new converts with those two passages," Samuel said.

When the haircut was finished, the man left, head bowed and thoughtful.

Samuel spent much time praying for his clients. When someone came to him for a haircut, especially if the person was a stranger, Samuel committed the encounter to the Holy Spirit's guidance. If an apparent opening for witness occurred but he did not feel comfortable about speaking, Samuel prolonged casual conversation, waiting for sure guidance.

Sometimes no further guidance came, but often it did.

Samuel wondered about the man who had spoken with him on the way to indoctrination class. It had been dark, and he had not gotten a good look at the man's face. The man had known that Samuel was a Christian and indicated that he wanted to talk to him.

Then one afternoon a client came. "About time for me to have a haircut," he said casually. He spoke like a ventriloquist, not moving his lips. Samuel restrained his joy, lest a guard take notice.

"I saw you in the field and at meals," the client said, "but the cadres have eyes that seldom wander. I determined one day I would find an excuse to be near you, using the little technique I have developed of speaking without lip movement. A man in my dormitory does the same. We have good times together. Now I come for a haircut in this secluded corner, and I find you as my barber!"

That day, to the rhythm of clipper and scissors, another prisoner entered the Good Shepherd's kingdom.

Months passed between letters from Sui Ling. She always wrote briefly, and with caution. She was a truly great woman, astute and wise. Ai Ling managed to visit Samuel three times before she left for Macau to get married. Guangzhou was much closer to Shao Guan than was Fushan, where Sui Ling lived in her father's home.

One day in 1960 during a lull, awaiting customers, Samuel received instructions to greet a visitor at the main hall. It was his sister Ai Ling. They had thirty delightful minutes together. Although they were watched constantly, they could talk privately. They sat at a table facing each other. How he wished Sui Ling might have obtained permission, but it was good seeing his sister.

Ai Ling described Samuel's children, their growth, their learning. She told him what she knew of Sui Ling. When Samuel asked about the Da Ma Zhan congregation, she told him it had disbanded. Samuel's heart missed a beat.

"Mother believes these are days of preparation for greater

things in China," Ai Ling said. "Even now, many are becoming Christians. Some fall away, but many are faithful and brave."

Soon the guard came to the table and gestured for Samuel's visitor to leave the room. Samuel watched Ai Ling leave and slowly went back to his cell.

Profound loneliness pressed on him, but he also felt intense joy because by his side, just as real as his sister's body had been, he sensed the continued abiding of the Presence.

12

WITH THE COMING of 1963 came the passing of nearly five of twenty years of imprisonment for Samuel Lamb. He experienced increasing freedom as the labor-camp barber. His cadre rarely inspected. He was on his own. He thanked God. Above all, he was building a congregation—a body of believers to whom he never preached, never served the Lord's Supper, and on whom he never called—but they looked to him as their spiritual leader.

As the months passed, he missed Sui Ling more and more. She was not able to visit him. Letters arrived once a month, if that. Samuel didn't have even a photograph of her or his children, only memories becoming ever more indistinct.

And yet when Samuel looked at the larger picture of his life, he saw himself uniquely situated in the place of his Lord's appointing. He was under a kind of house arrest. In prison terminology he was spoken of by some as "one of the commandant's boys."

A more accurate perspective of his situation focused the day he responded to a summons from the cadre in charge of indoctrination, an opportunist who saw his present post as a stop on the route to the higher rank he coveted and intended

101

to achieve. He targeted Samuel Lamb as a choice pawn in the game he played.

The cadre's success lay entirely in his role as an evangelist of his communist ideology. The further a prisoner was from this ideology, the more determined the cadre was to see the prisoner "liberated."

"Prisoner Lamb," he began, as Samuel took a seat in the man's austere office, "you have been commended by many of my peers." Samuel felt an impulse to express appreciation but judged silence to be the better response.

"You work diligently. You perform, on an average, five more daily haircuts than did your predecessor. And the quality of your work is superior to his. You have never been guilty of infractions of any kind. You follow prison rules in detail." He picked up a report sheet, which he now scanned for a silent interim. "But in your most important need, you seem to have made little progress, if any at all. Thus you have cost the government much expense, all loss, by not benefiting from our teaching."

He again paused. Samuel felt a tinge of apprehension. He wondered what they would do with an unprofitable learner like him.

The Presence whispered, "If any of you lacks wisdom . . ." Samuel claimed the promise once again, silently, earnestly.

"Why do you persist in your outmoded Christian beliefs?" the cadre pressed. Samuel searched for words but could find none. "Let me state the question a different way. You have been in the government's training program nearly a full five years. Over that period of time, do you see yourself giving consideration to the truths of Communism as opposed to the false bigotry of Christianity?"

If any of you lacks wisdom, Samuel repeated in his mind.

"Answer me!" he demanded.

Whoever disowns me before men, I will disown him before my Father in heaven, Samuel thought.

The affronted cadre slammed his fist onto the table as he sprang to his feet. "You will give me your answer!"

Samuel also stood. "Sir," he began, "I have an earthly

father. I may disown him or dishonor him, but he remains my earthly father. I cannot change that relationship. I also have a heavenly Father, whose love for me is more living and real than any earthly relationship. This is the most important fact of my entire life, a truth I could not deny under any circumstances."

The cadre was silent for several minutes, glaring at Samuel. Twice his lips moved in preparation for speech, but he refrained. Was he thinking that the unfruitful branch of a tree should be pruned and destroyed? With a wave of his hand, he signaled for Samuel to leave.

In the months that followed, Samuel's mobile barber service became a continuing site for evangelism and discipling. Prisoners who received spiritual help recommended the pastor barber to their friends. Sheer percentages increased the possibility that someone, sitting for a haircut and feigning sincerity, might report him to the commandant's office and bring him and his ministry into grave danger.

The Word of God became increasingly precious to Samuel as he struggled to retain every phrase and word he had memorized. He took great comfort in verses that spoke about the power and fruitfulness of God's Word: "As the rain and the snow come down from heaven, and do not return to it without watering the earth and making it bud and flourish, . . . so is my word that goes out from my mouth: It will not return to me empty but will accomplish what I desire and achieve the purpose for which I sent it."

With the passing of time, the precious words stored up in his mind became less distinct. If only he had a Bible, or even just a New Testament, to refresh his memory!

One morning a prisoner came to the barber's chair. "Are you new here?" Samuel asked.

"New," affirmed the stranger.

After clipping for several minutes, Samuel began subconsciously humming the gospel song "Rescue the Perishing."

At the third line of the stanza, the man in the chair joined audibly on the line, "Snatch them in pity from sin and the grave." Samuel dropped his scissors.

"We are both believers?" the man asked, extending his hand.

"We are!" Samuel exclaimed.

The man told him his name and said, "I was a pastor before my arrest."

"So was I!" responded Samuel. Footsteps approached. The two remained silent.

A prisoner came into view and asked, "How much longer?"

"Ten minutes," Samuel told him. He looked at his new friend and hastily added, "Make it fifteen!"

"I will be back," said the man and went on.

When they were alone, Samuel's new friend asked, "Do you have a Bible?"

"I haven't so much as seen one in five years," Samuel replied.

The man glanced cautiously about, then said softly, "I have a New Testament." Samuel dropped his scissors a second time.

"The New Testament?" he whispered. "How did you bring it in?"

"By the grace of God," the brother replied. "My cadre took it from me but then returned it. He is a man with a heart."

"A Bible!" Samuel whispered.

"Do you have pen and paper?"

"Would you let me copy from it?"

"Most gladly. I will bring it to you Saturday. You may then keep it for a few days."

"God bless and reward you!"

By this time, Samuel was earning a few *yuan* per month with which to purchase personal items. He went to buy some paper and a supply of pencils from the commissary. "Nobody ever bought so much paper before," the prisoner in charge said. "I'm not sure if you are getting more than is policy. Whatever will you do with so much?"

"I have many things that I need to remember."

"A diary? I have often thought to do the same."

Samuel paid for the paper and found a place in the shadows. His many weeks of barbering had shown him a number of quiet nooks in which to work with measured privacy.

He began with the gospel of John: "In the beginning was the Word, and the Word was with God, and the Word was God. . . ." On and on he read and copied, through the night and into the dawn.

At the breakfast bell he hurried to mess. He made himself visible at times through the day, but as often as he dared, he sought out his project area.

By Tuesday he had completed the gospel of John. He considered copying one of the other gospels next, but decided instead on the book of Acts. How beautiful, every word! "When they saw the courage of Peter and John and realized they were unschooled, ordinary men, they were astonished and they took note that these men had been with Jesus." When Samuel Lamb read these words from Acts 4, he realized that the same Jesus who had been with Peter and John was now with him.

His courage rose as by Sunday night he was well into the book of Revelation. His fingers ached, and numbness tinged his wrist as he found a secure place for the book and retired to the dormitory.

Every spare moment in the next week he worked on his project. He was overjoyed to find concepts he had forgotten, ideas in the New Testament story he hadn't seen before, shades of meaning fresh to his spirit—the words flowed onto his paper.

One night when all the others slept, he crept through the shadows to a secluded corner. The faint rays of a security light outside a dirty window barely provided enough light for Samuel to read the small words on the pages.

Word on word, laboriously, he continued the transcription. "Holy, holy, holy is the Lord God Almighty, who was, and is, and is to come."

"Prisoner!" A nightwatch cadre stood over him! "What are you writing?" the cadre demanded.

Not waiting for a reply, the cadre snatched the New Testament and the sheaf of copies. In that moment the dim overhanging bulb seemed like a searchlight. "I'll take these to the commandant's office," the cadre said in a huff.

Not only did Samuel lose the borrowed New Testament and his newly copied chapters, but he also lost his position as camp barber. He was transferred to an intensive re-education team consisting of incorrigibles from various areas. They were the "rotten" group.

This group was required to sit through not two hours of indoctrination but eight, ten, and twelve hours a day—for six months. Samuel's mind grew weary, his soul distressed, but his faith strengthened. As the teaching cadre droned on about the merits of communism, Samuel would repeat in his mind the Scripture passages he had just studied in his short refresher course: *In this you greatly rejoice, though now for a little while you may have had to suffer grief in all kinds of trials. These have come so that your faith—of greater worth than gold, which perishes even though refined by fire—may be proved genuine.*

"We are determined to rid you of your bad thinking," the teaching cadre told the group. But Samuel stood resolutely by his faith.

Then, in July 1963, he was taken with five hundred other prisoners to a train siding. Men had heard rumors that they were bound for a coal mine in Shansi province.

"We are no longer prisoners," grumbled one of the men. "If you ask me, I think the government needs cheap labor and who better than us?"

"I hear there are over three thousand men at the site where we're going," said another.

Three thousand men! As the train, heavy with human freight, labored slowly on toward the north, Samuel prayed, "Let me touch those who seek for you!"

They were headed for Taiyuan, in the heart of Shansi province's abundant coal fields, immediately below Inner Mongolia, to the far north.

13

SAMUEL ARRIVED in Shanxi on July 21, 1963. He spent the first six months in intensive reeducation. It was the same diatribe: "In class society, without exception, thinking is stamped with the brand of that class. . . . All reactionaries are paper tigers. In appearance, the reactionaries are terrifying. In reality, they are powerless. . . . The communist party does not fear criticism because the truth is on our side."

The cadres in Shanxi had Samuel Lamb's records from Shao Guan, so they knew of his religious bias. The difference, however, was that at Shao Guan he had been an exception, one of a few. He now sat in lectures with men who also had been rejected for their contrariness, the lot of them categorized as "rotten dissidents." University lecturers, scientists, journalists, manufacturers, bankers, entrepreneurs, landlords, men of influence, men of wealth—all innately were opposed to Communism. All were prize candidates for "conversion" and "rehabilitation."

At Shao Guan, self-criticism sessions had been imposed. However, the men could generalize and still be approved. Criticism was also encouraged at the Shanxi camp, but because the classes involved large groups of men, in-depth participation was not practical.

The longer Samuel stood victim to the mind-molding and mind-controlling methods of Communism, the more clearly he discerned how atheism desecrated and adapted God's methods for its own evil purposes. The Bible assures us that "If we confess our sins, he is faithful and just and will forgive us our sins and purify us from all unrighteousness."

Jesus Christ—Creator and Savior of the human family. In contrast, Mao Zedong—architect and rescuer of human society.

One message came through clearly to Samuel Lamb: Christians must never use the tainted methodology of the Communists. But, if God spared him and gave him some years of freedom to preach and teach, he determined to be no less zealous in winning and molding of human hearts for the glory of God. If God spared him.

Fifteen years of incarceration yet remained for this frail and gentle man, and he soon had reason to suspect he would see heaven before he saw so much as a mile of freedom leading away from the coal mines of Shanxi. In January 1964, Samuel Lamb was loaded onto a transport trailer and was taken to the mouth of a large coal mine. Locomotive-pushed-and-drawn cars provided transport for both men and mineral, since the tunnels into the mine's rich belly went horizontally, not vertically.

All through the long working day, prisoners worked in a stooped position. Although Samuel's short stature was for once an advantage to him in the low mine, his limited strength brought him into crisis the very first day.

The strenuous work in the mine made the most debilitating work at Shao Guan seem easy by comparison. Even when he worked with another person, the digging and loading of the slabs strained his muscles beyond endurance.

No psychological testing identified and isolated those who suffered from claustrophobia. Often Samuel would hear anguished cries nearby or echoed, ghostlike cries from the distance. Several men were injured that first day, setting a pattern that continued day after day.

The cadres followed orders not to inflict physical punishment, but they expected every prisoner to extend himself to the utmost of his strength and stamina. For diminutive Samuel, with a physique scarcely the shadow of others, days grew excruciatingly long and exhausting. His physical weakness was made worse by the mockery he endured from the larger and stronger men. He was weakened not only by the physical labor but also by coal dust, which seeped into his lungs every minute of the day.

Each man brought his own lunch, often tasteless rice with a piece of tough, dried meat and vegetables reminiscent of the swill that nourished the swine at Shao Guan. The quantity of food was sufficient, for the bosses knew their hostage work force needed to sustain energy. But no one gave any thought to how the food would taste to the men. If a unit lagged behind in producing the day's demanded output, prisoners would eat while they worked. Food frequently dropped to the dust-grime of the mine floor, but hungry men learned to spit out the ore and swallow the food.

The prisoners were amateurs, not seasoned miners. They made mistakes. They became bruised by falling coal. Utterly exhausted from the day's work, they had little energy for camaraderie and conversation. Sometimes the air was more filthy with cursing than with dust. These were the utterly condemned, men destined for years of toil in the earth's rank bowels.

However, faith in God and confidence in the Scriptures sustained the silenced Guangzhou pastor. It pained him to have so little opportunity for witness. Yet, he knew he was in the sharpest focus of the very eye of God. Although he had never memorized the book of Job, he knew it well. And he drew comfort, strength, and guidance from Job's experiences.

"He knows the way that I take; when he has tested me, I will come forth as gold." Job could say it. And so could Samuel Lamb!

He became more vividly aware of the Presence. And although his copied pages of Scripture had been confiscated,

110 | Ken Anderson

those long hours of copying had functioned as a refresher course in the New Testament. Clear in his mind were the pain and ignominies Jesus suffered. When an avalanche of ore fell on his head and shoulders, he thought of Stephen. When lights failed on another occasion and he stood in total darkness, he thought about the blind man and the Great Physician's touch that brought him from utter darkness to glorious light.

During those years of China's foment, the coal mines of Shanxi lay a world apart from Samuel's family in Guangzhou. Family visits were neither possible nor allowed. Mail arrived sparingly. The depths of the coal mine became a taunting symbol of the distance separating him from his wife and family. But the Presence remained.

Had not David the psalmist who sang through adversity, declared: "He shall give his angels charge over thee, to keep thee in all thy ways"?

Assuredly he had. Assuredly and hallelujah!

In retrospect, Samuel says, "The Lord sustained me in a way I could have known only through experience. I now, in fullest sincerity, thank Him for that experience. I never knew a day when I was unaware of His love and mercy, never a time when I doubted or despaired. I knew my Lord was with me. I sensed my guardian angel ever at my side." The Presence assured him that "The eternal God is your refuge, and underneath are the everlasting arms."

After an exhausting day in the mine, Samuel spent a minimum of two hours listening to lectures. Beyond that, he had to memorize many pages of teaching, such as the writings of Marx and Lenin. By the conclusion of nightly lectures and required assignments, he was so exhausted that he often fell into bed without removing his clothes. He would try to review memorized Scripture as mental therapy that would quiet his mind from the strain of heretical dogma, but he invariably fell asleep in the middle of a verse or promise.

One morning above the din of a narrow gauge tram that carried the prisoners into the mine, he whispered, "Forgive me, Lord, if in my weariness I neglect your Word! Help me to gain strength as a Christian, not to weaken."

It was on such a day he began perfecting a skill that he had practiced at Shao Guan and before. Samuel learned to *work and pray*, much as Jesus had taught his disciples to *watch and pray*. While wielding pick and shovel, while hoisting cumbersome slabs of ore, he prayed for his family, for the disintegrating congregation back in Guangzhou. God gave him love for the cadres, for government officials. He prayed for Three-Self, blessing the names of those who had oppressed him.

His mole-like confinement gave him a new perspective of China. The land and its people were shut out from his view, yet he became keenly sensitive to his nation and its people.

Infrequent letters from home included Scripture inferences that told him of Christians suffering in Guangzhou and in other parts of China. "Suffering produces perseverance; perseverance, character; and character, hope." He sensed that God was using these sufferings to shape his church in China: "Our light and momentary troubles are achieving for us an eternal glory." With new insight, he saw persecution as preparation—for individuals, for the whole of Christ's body.

Was God preparing China's church for future service? For ministry to itself and outward to the world in ways unique for all time? Samuel became increasingly convinced it was so.

How much better, at the rending of the skies for Messiah's soon advent, to find a church in pursuit of spiritual excellence rather than a church cancered by secularism and complacency!

Mercifully, Samuel's supervisors saw not only his physical limitations but also the consistent effort he made to shoulder his share of work. They saw how his daily effort, extended beyond his vitality and endurance, sapped his strength like a disease, so they assigned him to the responsibility of uncoupling empty cars and recoupling loads of ore—a task requiring agility rather than physical strength.

Again God answered prayer. "You prepare a table before

me in the presence of my enemies," he whispered in gratitude as he ate his lunch in a nearly dust-free area.

Samuel's new responsibilities gave him long periods of time alone with interims of busy, pressured time, but he was free to sing, free to quote Scripture, free to pray aloud.

He cherished two Scripture passages, both of them written in prison—to the Christians at Philippi, to understudy Timothy, and to Samuel Lamb:

> Do not be anxious about anything, but in everything, by prayer and petition, with thanksgiving, present your requests to God. And the peace of God, which transcends all understanding, will guard your hearts and minds in Christ Jesus.

> I have fought the good fight, I have finished the race, I have kept the faith. Now there is in store for me the crown of righteousness, which the Lord, the righteous Judge, will award to me on that day—and not only to me, but also to all who have longed for his appearing.

The position as car coupler brought numerous other people to Samuel. To many he gave his witness. To some he introduced the Savior.

Often cars came on line so quickly that he had to work at top speed. It could be nerve-racking. Some men lost fingers, hands, even their lives.

"I got a small scratch once," he muses.

One day, owing to a malfunction for which Samuel was not responsible, a loaded coal car careened down the track and loomed toward him like a missile aimed at his destruction. For a moment he anticipated certain death. He felt himself wrapped in glowing peace. He thought, *How wonderful to be soon in my Lord's presence!*

Presence? Ah, yes, *the* Presence! As he watched the car hurling toward him, he thought about the promise: *He shall give his angels charge over thee, to keep thee in all thy ways.* As if restrained by the supra-muscled arm of an angel, the car stopped, pinning Samuel firmly but unharmed to the wall of the mine. Exclamations of praise preceded his calls for help.

That day the Lord reminded Samuel of the apostle Paul's word to the Corinthians: "God is faithful; he will not let you be tempted beyond what you can bear. But when you are tempted, he will also provide a way out so that you can stand up under it." One of the other men in the mine was killed instantly in a similar situation.

Death by accident happened all too frequently, while others became so depressed that they resorted to suicide.

Samuel had opportunities to witness to desperate men. He often met prisoners who evidenced various stages of depression. He met others who were crippled by fear. "If you spend the remainder of your life in the mine," he exhorted them, becoming more effective in one-on-one evangelism, "it is only a moment compared to the darkness of an eternity without God."

"No guards watch you," one man said to Samuel.

Samuel laughed. "I cannot dig my way out, can I?"

The other man also laughed. "I haven't laughed in a month," he said.

"'A cheerful heart is good medicine,' the Bible says. To the Christian, our faith is always sufficient for whatever our need may be!" The mention of faith and the Bible gave opportunity for one miner's lips to console and counsel another miner's heart.

With the unrelenting ban on initiating any form of evangelism, Samuel's constant prayer was for openings. When they came, he always nurtured the opportunity with care, knowing that effort might be made at any time to ensnare him.

One of those whom Samuel admonished was Lai Tin Kay, a student sent to the mine to quiet his intellectual zeal. "Life has lost all purpose for me," he told Samuel. "I wanted to do what other students here have done. I would have killed myself if I had not met you and found you sustained by an inner strength. What is the source of this strength?"

During a lull in the work, they were alone. Samuel rolled a fallen slab beside another as he gestured for both to sit. "We come into the world incomplete," he said. "We can attain many values within ourselves, as you seem to have done, but provision for our greatest need cannot be self-generated. It cannot be found within us. It must come from outside us."

"How do you have such sure faith?" Lai asked.

"I, in myself, have no faith."

"But—"

"Remember, I said that provision for a person's greatest need must come from outside. It cannot be self-generated."

"This is the case with faith?"

"Yes. The Bible tells us that 'faith cometh by hearing, and hearing by the word of God.'"

Thereupon, Samuel Lamb led Lai Tin Kay through a step-by-step awareness of the gospel message—the sinfulness of all men, the death and resurrection of Jesus Christ, the declaration of Scripture that "the wages of sin is death, but the gift of God is eternal life in Christ Jesus our Lord."

Others came with hearts hungering, minds open, wills bent toward finding this external and eternal supply. If he were not in this mine, Samuel pondered, would there have been anyone to point the way?

Samuel daily sensed his own faith grow. He not only learned to accept the coal mine and his lengthy sentence, but he also probed more deeply the words of Paul to his Philippian friends, "I have learned the secret of being content in any and every situation." Testing had brought him to this point.

As the years ebbed slowly past, he missed his family increasingly. He would sit alone in the mine during lull periods, close his eyes, and imagine himself at home—with Sui Ling, with the children, with his mother and sisters.

Sui Ling's letters came infrequently, then none at all. This troubled him, yet he knew how painful it might be for her to write, how she might reason that her letters would be more painfully received than if none came to him at all.

Yet all of this was part of testing, and Samuel Lamb could thank God for clouds as well as sunshine. He had an intense perception of life's brevity during the coal mine years, and he saw the more clearly the right of the Good

Shepherd to permit whatever he chose in the process of molding the faith of his children.

Samuel Lamb praised God. He wondered at the magnitude of grace that could take a weak mortal such as himself to such an uplifted plane.

But what of others of God's children, those who lived within the reach of ease, those who could take freedom for granted, those who prayed only when they were in deepest fear and adversity?

He would not exchange his circumstances for theirs.

14

YEAR TWENTY BEGAN. In the years preceding 1974
through 1977, Samuel had received commendations for
service and attitude. One Chinese New Year, the cadres gave
him a fountain pen as a memento of exemplary status. In the
case of some offenders this could have meant reduction of
sentence.

Not so for Prisoner Lamb.

He had been given high marks for conduct, to be sure, but
bottom rank in the cleansing of thought and reorientation of
objectives.

Along the whispered corridors of the mine came reports of
men who, after completing their sentences, were not permitted to return home. Some were sent to cities and areas far
removed from their roots. Others were inducted into forced
labor.

Samuel knew that the government's objective was for
parolees to return home as trophies of those whose thinking
had been corrected. He wondered if his sentence would be
indefinitely extended because he had made no ideological
progress.

In late May 1978, however, he was summoned to headquarters, where one of the cadres told him he was on the list of imminent discharge. That was joyful news, to be sure. However, on May 29, he was sent back to the mine. Were they toying with him, he wondered, cat and captive? *Were they retaliating because he had refused to denounce his Christian faith?*

"I cried to the Lord for deliverance," he says. "My faith laid desperate hold on my Good Shepherd's many promises."

He was sent deep into the mine, terrain he had not seen in eight years. He felt as if he were reliving those initial days.

"You new?" one of the miners asked.

"To the contrary," Samuel responded, "I'm scheduled for release."

The man laughed. "Not if they send you back into the mine," he said.

The old weariness and the nagging debility returned. For a full week Samuel labored as he had done in his initial year. Then one night, while he was in line for the night's meal, pain struck his back like the sudden thrust of a knife. He was taken to the medical ward. A doctor of his approximate age stepped up to the bed. Refreshingly cordial, the doctor asked, "Mine injury?"

"No," Samuel responded.

The doctor eyed him skeptically for a moment, then took up the chart from the end of the bed. "I congratulate you," he said. "You are listed as exemplary. You are unlikely to feign illness to get out of the mine."

The doctor made preliminary examination. "I can't find the source of your pain," he said. "We'll give you an injection so you can sleep. Tomorrow we'll probe further."

Tests provided no decisive diagnosis. Samuel remained in bed for a few days, the pain subsiding. With time to think, his mind drifted homeward. He had heard nothing from his wife in more than a year. And his family had not mentioned her in any of their letters. It was unthinkable that she would wait for him nearly two decades only to forsake him.

Yet why had she not written? He could only assume that her letters had not reached him.

One positive aspect of Samuel's prison years was his insulation from the devastating Cultural Revolution between the years 1966 and 1976. Mao's Red Guard, known as the *Hong Wei Bing*, had had their blood and brains set afire in 1966, when the chairman convened fourteen million young people in Tienanmen Square. He convinced them that China would be a workers' paradise in which all intellectuals were suspect. Then he sent them plundering across China. They vandalized the nation's most precious art treasures, slaughtered over one million people, and left multitudes maimed from merciless beatings. Adapting an old idiom, they liked to say, "We cut off the dog's tail an inch at a time."

But things did not happen according to Mao's plan. The chairman's initial intent was for the young zealots to humble party cadres who had grown soft and fat from their years in power. Instead, the *Hong Wei Bing* became the *liu-mang*, the Chinese word for "tough kids." Red Guard mobs devastated schools and instigated the demeaning and imprisonment of professors and schoolmasters. Churches and individual Christians also fell prey to the ruthless mob.

Thousands of homes were invaded, left in shambles. Family art treasures were destroyed. Books and cultural items were burned in the streets. In the residences of Christians, frenzied young zealots searched for Bibles, Christian literature, hymnbooks, wall mottoes—anything they deemed religious—to add fuel to their public fires.

The Red Guards would interrupt a Sunday-morning worship service and command the communicants to smash stained-glass windows. Then the Guards would force the pastor and his family to carry out hymnbooks and Bibles, tear out the pages one by one, and throw them into the fire. Back in the sanctuary, the church members were forced to brick up the openings left by the smashed glass.

The young brigands did not spare Three-Self churches. TSPM clergy went to labor camps—their churches desecrated, and their members reduced to the same ignominy of others.

During this era of cultural and spiritual demolition, China was smitten with "not a famine of food or a thirst for water, but a famine of hearing the words of the LORD," as the shepherd Amos had prophesied for Israel. Missionary radio stations—such as Trans-World Radio and the Far East Broadcasting Company—beamed the Scriptures back across the Bamboo Curtain. Christians who owned shortwave radios sat by the hour copying lengthy, slow, and precise dictation of God's Word.

Ignominy befell not only pastors and lay Christians. Literature and art dating back to antiquity fed street bonfires. Intellectuals, musicians, writers, and teachers were forced to wear dunce caps and parade in the streets. Deng Pufang, son of China's premier at the time of the Tienanmen Square trauma, was assaulted for being a student at Beijing University. Red Guards threw him out of a second-floor window, dooming young Deng to life in a wheelchair.

Schools were, in fact, closed throughout the country. Students between the ages of fifteen and thirty-five were denied education and sent to the countryside. It is estimated that as many as 100 million young people became common laborers instead of realizing their goals of serving China as doctors, teachers, lawyers, or civic and national leaders. Those ten years marked the end of the Mao era and virtually denied him forever the place in history he had so ardently coveted.

Samuel, insulated from China's tumult, knew little-to-nothing of the carnage and plunder. He anticipated his release from prison with a certain amount of apprehension, wondering how much he would recognize from the China of twenty years past.

On an unforgettable day Samuel received notification from the commandant's office that his sentence neared conclusion and that his clearance was being processed. His heart was full of joy, and quickened with excitement.

Then in May, a telegram came from his sister.

MOTHER IS SERIOUSLY ILL. MUST COME SOON TO
SEE HER ALIVE. AI LING

He had gone twenty years without the counsel and support of this saintly woman. Letters from home had told of her waning years. He had often opened letters, wondering if they would say she had died. Now he sensed the Good Shepherd's timing. He would see his mother once more, hear her voice, share her prayers. Awareness of her prayers and the prayers of his wife and sisters had been balm and buttress to his spirits through these two decades of separation.

Then in the middle of May the cadre in charge of his group summoned him to his office and said bluntly, "You will not be approved for return to Guangzhou."

"But my wife is there!" he protested. "My children! I received a wire telling me my mother is dying!"

The cadre waved his hand to move on. Samuel's spirits plummeted. Yet he understood. Model prisoner, he may have been. Model student of the new ideologies, he was not. Now the time of reckoning had come. Discipleship demanded its price, well he knew. He had dared to think that the endless years of incarceration would be sum enough.

"It is difficult to imagine, Prisoner Lamb," one of the teaching cadres had said. "You have sat under our instruction for two decades. We have carefully explained to you the superiority of Marxist ideology. Yet you persist in labeling yourself a Christian." Samuel wondered if his release had been blocked by the officials' need to save face.

Guangzhou was one of China's most strategic cities, a world trade center. The government would want to deter the influence of a man who so unflinchingly opposed the tenets of Communism and affirmed Christianity as superior to the doctrines of Lenin and Marx.

From a prison in Rome the apostle Paul had instructed the Christians at Ephesus to "sing and make music in your heart to the Lord, always giving thanks to God the Father for everything." But how could Samuel give thanks?

Even more convincingly, Paul had told his friends in Thessalonica: "Give thanks in all circumstances, for this is God's will for you in Christ Jesus."

In *all* circumstances? Merciful Lord! How could Samuel Lamb give thanks? How could anyone?

"You will be released," one of the other cadres told

him, "but not to Guangzhou." As if wishing to extend encouragement, the cadre added, "Possibly Beijing or Shanghai. I have no idea, of course."

Samuel's pulse quickened at the mention of Shanghai. Perhaps Wang Mingdao was still alive and was still ministering. Perhaps Wang Mingdao would have a place for him to share. Perhaps Sui Ling could join him in Shanghai! Prisoners knew, of course, that rigid travel restrictions could detain a man at whatever site the government decreed.

One night, preparing for bed, Samuel overheard two others talking nearby. "When is your release date?" asked one.

The other man replied, "I only know it will be soon and that it will be back to Guangzhou."

"Guangzhou!" Samuel uttered aloud.

He crawled into bed and drew the blanket up above his eyes.

A few days later he again suffered back pains. "I find nothing organically wrong," the doctor told him. He was refreshingly congenial. "You are due for release soon. Your subconscious must be skipping dances of joy up and down your backbone." Ordinarily, Samuel would have been amused. But he hadn't been able to force a smile since his chat with the cadre about release.

"Ah, so that's it!" The doctor studied Samuel's face a long moment. "You have had bad news." Samuel looked at the floor. "Well, I'm not a psychiatrist, but telling me might help." Samuel hesitated. "But only if you wish to."

"I received a cable. My mother is near death."

"Perhaps she will linger long enough—"

"I have been told I am not being returned to Guangzhou."

The doctor shook his head in an expression of sincere empathy. He looked about cautiously. "I have been a loyal citizen all through these troubled years," he said, "but I wonder if the government isn't driving such a wedge between itself and our people."

He hesitated and was about to continue speaking as Samuel added, "I have put it all into God's hands."

The doctor's attitude instantly changed. "God's hands?" His voice was like a clap of thunder. He obviously did not mind who might overhear. "So that's it! Religious paranoia! You still suck the breasts of dead superstitions. No wonder your back is in knots!"

It was mosquito season again. That night, nestled under the netting that overhung his hospital bed, Samuel Lamb struggled to his knees and drew himself into the position of a boy at evening prayers. "Please, heavenly Father," he interceded quietly, "I claim every promise of your blessing. I ask you to perform a miracle and clear the orders for me to return home."

Another convalescent, who had previously seen and heard him at prayer in this manner, called out, "Stomach cramps again, Lamb?" Others saw Samuel on his knees and laughed. Samuel stretched out onto his cot, drew the blanket over his head, and continued praying.

15

JUNE 14, 1978.

Prisoner Samuel Lamb was summoned to penitentiary headquarters. "Here are your discharge papers" said one of the cadres, handing him an official envelope.

With trembling fingers Samuel opened the envelope and took out the papers: an official termination of sentence, the beginning of a five-year probation, a small sum of money—and a one-way ticket to Guangzhou! He felt like Jacob hearing the news of Joseph in Egypt. And he understood a bit of the emotions that Abraham felt when the angel forbade him to end the life of his son.

The next day Samuel joined a group of released prisoners who journeyed to nearby Taiyuan. They walked the streets, looked in the shop windows, and strolled through parks.

Not until early July did travel documents finalize for his group to board trains for passage to assigned destinations. Samuel took his place with trembling anticipation.

Every mile he traveled south heightened the temperature outside and inside the train. The packed train cars took on a climate of their own, hotter than the steaming countryside and humid from the rancid perspiration of bodies cramped together.

Belching a continual plume of smoke from coal that Samuel himself might have grubbed out of the mine, the train traveled through fertile Henan, crossed the swollen Yangtse at Hankow, on and ever downward through Jiangxi to enter at last Samuel's own province of Guangdong.

On July 17, as the train creaked and puffed into Guangzhou station, Samuel Lamb glanced at his watch. It was 7:40 in the morning.

Sui Ling, his mother, his sisters, and his children . . . His heart pounded like a drum when he thought about them. "I felt like a stranger in my own surroundings," he says. "I trembled and felt numb. Twenty years had not brought great physical change to the city, with the stalemate incited by the Cultural Revolution, but two decades had certainly dimmed my recollections."

Then slowly he began to get his bearings. Bus 119. Yes, that was it. Out of the deep recesses of his memory it came. And there was a 119 just now, pulling away from the station. The next would be his, his to the gateway entry of Da Ma Zhan street.

He breathed a prayer of praise from the Psalms: "You are mighty, O Lord, and your faithfulness surrounds you." Hallelujah!

No one recognized him as he stepped off the bus at Zhong Shan 5 and entered Da Ma Zhan. He thought he remembered some faces, but wasn't sure. Even the shops and residence doorways appeared at most only vaguely familiar. But not 35 Da Ma Zhan—he caught sight of it ten shops away! Weary though he was, aching yet from the long journey, he walked more briskly.

Then he stopped. What was this? It was residence 35 but with the entrance locked shut. Locked from the outside.

"Sui Ling," he whispered. "My mother, my family." Had something happened to them?

Then he saw that an alternate entrance stood open, an entry to the upper floor. He walked slowly to the open entrance and began to ascend.

"Someone is coming," he heard a voice say. His sister Ai Ling appeared at the upper level above the stairs. She stood a moment in curious silence. She could not make out her brother's face against the glare of the bright street.

"I am home," Samuel managed to say.

"Oh!" his sister gasped. "It's Samuel! Samuel! Samuel!" She took his arm and led him into the living quarters the family had established on the second floor of their property. The touch of her hand felt strange to one who had experienced no physical affection or cordiality in two decades.

"We live only upstairs now," Ai Ling managed to say. "The Red Guards drove us out of the ground floor, and the government confiscated our property, but they left us this second level." They moved now toward a doorway on the property's street side. Samuel remembered that it was his mother's bedroom.

"Mother?" he questioned cautiously.

"Mother is in here," Ai Ling said, moving them through the doorway, into the presence of a bedridden, emaciated woman.

"Mother," Samuel's lips formed but scarcely spoke.

"Ai Ling," the woman called out weakly. "Who is this old man?"

"It's Samuel," Ai Ling told her. "He has returned this day from prison—your son, my brother."

There was a moment tense with silence. Outside, a hawker's call filtered up through the window. An airplane droned overhead, moving into Guangzhou's busy landing pattern.

"Samuel?" The old woman's wavering voice broke the silence, not in disbelief but in emotional shock.

"Mother!" Samuel called back to her.

The aged matriarch held out her hands. Samuel and Ai Ling bounded together into her arms. The three gasped out their love to each other, their gratitude to God. Then, with faltering strength, the old woman gently pushed back her son to see him better. Ai Ling brought her mother's eyeglasses.

"It is! It is you, my son! God has brought you back! I can go to him now! I have again seen my son!"

A metallic sound came into the room. Samuel at first did not turn, so intent he was to look at his mother. "Is this my grandpa?" a small boy's voice asked. Samuel turned.

"We have told him about you since he was in our arms," Ai Ling said.

In the excitement of the moment, Samuel had forgotten the letters in which he had learned of his daughter Hannah's marriage and the birth of a grandson. Samuel's eyes widened. A finger touched his lips as he stood.

"Sui Ling?" he asked. "Is she in Fushan with her family?"

Ai Ling looked at her brother for a long moment as she attempted to speak. But she could say nothing.

"Tomorrow is Friday, is it not? Will she come at the weekend? Could we get a message to her?" Ai Ling remained silent.

"Sui Ling and Hannah and Enoch?" Samuel prompted in apprehension.

"We thought to write to you," the sister finally began, "but Mother asked why add hurt to the weight of your suffering." Unable to any longer suppress her emotions, Ai Ling began to weep.

"Tell me!" Samuel cried out as he grasped his sister's arm. Ai Ling looked up. "Is she—?" Samuel prompted.

Ai Ling nodded. "A year ago," she managed to say.

"She is with Jesus," Samuel's mother said weakly. "Glory to God! As soon your mother shall be!"

Samuel turned, walked out of the room, and stumbled alone to the opposite end of the dwelling. He had never in his lifetime anguished as he anguished in those moments. The expanse of the prison years had been no more cruel and ominous than the stifling of hope and joy that now came across his mind like a canopy of hopelessness. But even in this time of near-despair he realized the long incarceration had prepared him for such as this—for the disappointments of this today, and for the demands of the tomorrows.

"The LORD gave and the LORD has taken away," the

sorrowing man whispered. "Blessed be the name of the LORD."

Somehow, in a dimension new and stimulating to him, he had never been more aware of the wisdom and goodness of his Lord.

His Lord . . .

And Sui Ling's!

16

SAMUEL'S MOTHER SURVIVED for nearly a year, slowly eaten away by lung cancer, but never losing the radiance of her soul. She was a warrior in prayer, tenacious in faith, and gentle in spirit. Although she required care, she blessed all her helpers with the glow of her celestial citizenship. In her unselfishness, she wished to have been taken in place of Sui Ling.

Samuel sensed ever more deeply that his two decades of imprisonment had been an era of preparation. He was schooled for a future that in the Sovereign One's plan might well exclude calm family life.

Friends cautioned Samuel of Three-Self scrutiny, which had resumed the moment he had stepped off the train at Guangzhou station. He heard rumors that other men who had languished in prison for decades had been sent back to prison for no known reason.

As a result, Samuel kept a low profile during the second half of 1978. He wondered daily about the growing congregation that had slowly dispersed over the twenty years, but he could hardly bring himself to call together such a group even were it feasible to do so. It was a time of transition, a time for acclimation.

For that matter, what if he were to face an audience on the next Lord's day? Or a study class some evening soon? He had lived without a Bible and study materials for so long that he felt like a novice again. When the Red Guards had sacked the Lamb residence, they took all Bibles, all of Samuel's considerable library and materials as well as his sermon and teaching notes. The seven booklets of the *Spiritual Collections* also had been taken and burned—from the Lamb bookshelves as well as from the homes of others who had obtained copies of their pastor's writings.

However, Ai Ling had been able to secure a copy of the entire Bible from a small TSPM bookroom. Samuel sat reading by the hour, his total self captivated by the depth and delight of reading the words of the living God, almost as if he were reading them for the first time. The Book ministered to him with clarity and vitality beyond what he had ever experienced. "When your words came, I ate them; they were my joy and my heart's delight!"

At times he wanted to take to the streets, to walk along Da Ma Zhan and out onto teeming Zhong Shan, Bible in hand, reading aloud for all to hear. "Show me, O LORD, my life's end and the number of my days; let me know how fleeting is my life. You have made my days a mere handbreadth; the span of my years is as nothing to you. Each man's life is but a breath."

He wondered why most people were ignorant of the Word of God. He wondered why God's children themselves sometimes grew indifferent toward the message from heaven. And he wondered what he could do to awaken and challenge and guide.

It was not fear that made him reticent to become an overt witness. It was reality: Aggressive evangelism and witnessing continued to be forbidden. And his prison record followed him like a condemning shadow. After twenty years of indoctrination, the government had failed to convince him to turn from his faith. Dare he affront a nation by proclaiming the reality of God in the face of avowed atheism?

"O Lord," he prayed, "don't let me live out the remainder of my days in silence!"

Then came December 4, 1978. He received a summons to appear at one of the offices of government registry. When he first read the summons, he experienced the old apprehension, but he didn't need to fear. For that day Samuel Lamb, the felon who had been stripped of all his rights, received the recertification of his citizenship!

Growing bolder, he resumed English classes the next month at 35 Da Ma Zhan. His students were mostly Christians, and at the time provided Samuel with little thought of a restored and growing congregation. He was finding his way back to civilian status. He knew God was leading him, but he had no grand visions of where.

Then three events signaled the restoration of Samuel Lamb's previous ministry. In the week before Sunday, March 25, 1979, he received a quiet invitation to conduct services at a home on Sing Feng Road. Believers in the area wished to establish a place of worship—an "illegal" house church.

"O Samuel!" his sister cautioned. "Do you dare?"

"They are also showing courage," Samuel replied. He searched his heart in those moments. How many times in the depths of a coal mine had he reminisced about the days when he stood before a group of believers to expound the Scriptures? What joy had once been his, looking into the countenance of an unbeliever and seeing the gleam of eternal life appear! Was he only curious to again experience such wonders, or was this surely the direction of the Holy Spirit?

He remembered Paul's words to the Corinthian church: "A great door for effective work has opened to me, and there are many who oppose me." What if Paul had declined to enter that door?

"I will go," Samuel told his sister. He hesitated, seeing her reticence. "I will go because I must."

"What do I tell Mother if she asks where you are?"

"Tell her the truth."

Out of discretion, not shame, Samuel carried his Bible in a small cloth market bag that Sunday morning. A dozen people gathered in a squalid flat above a shop. Common folk they were. Most had anguished under the Red Guards. All knew the incessant ache of deprivation. Because they were members of the labor classes, none had gone to prison or been dispatched to rural communes, but all were aware of the twenty-one years Samuel had spent in prison.

As Samuel entered the room, a muted awe came over them. Even in that first moment of resumed ministry, this modest man was looked on as a compatriot to the beleaguered saints of all ages.

Samuel led them in quiet singing. How good it was, directing a song service—any song service!

> Cast your burden on the Lord,
> Only lean upon His Word;
> You will soon have cause to bless
> His eternal faithfulness.

As Samuel spoke to that first small group, his little congregation knew a policeman could enter at any moment. Even though they numbered fewer than thirty-five, the stipulated quantity of illegal assembly, they realized that to meet, they were taking a great risk.

If Samuel Lamb had similar apprehensions, he gave no indication. In those moments the old glow returned, and his public preaching skills began to awaken from twenty years of disuse.

As a result of that Sunday-morning experience, a church was planted. The couple who had invited the group to assemble caught the vision Samuel shared, and they themselves led the meetings after that time.

For Samuel a second event indicated the Good Shepherd's continued guidance toward ministry. As a result of that initial Sunday experience, he began to think about resumption of worship at 35 Da Ma Zhan. He needed the seven booklets he had written in the *Spiritual Collections* series. One of these, "Baptism and the Lord's Supper," would be especially helpful if he were to resume leadership of a congregation. Could he perhaps rewrite the material?

Even as he considered such a procedure, he wondered

if he could recapture the essence of what he had written over two decades ago. Would he be able to recall the pertinent Scripture passages he had used?

Then one day, Zhu Feng, a former member of the disbanded 35 Da Ma Zhan congregation, came to visit Samuel. Samuel didn't recognize him at first. The visitor produced a small package and handed it to Samuel.

When Samuel opened the package, he found copies of the *Spiritual Collections* booklets! Zhu Feng told him how helpful the booklets had been in his Christian growth. After Samuel had been arrested and Zhu Feng could no longer sit under his preaching and teaching, the simple man had studied the booklets and had nearly memorized them. "I shared my learnings with others," he said.

Zhu Feng went on to tell Samuel how he had saved the booklets from the iconoclastic madness of the Red Guards in 1966. At night Zhu Feng had placed the booklets in an urn used for the bones and ashes of deceased ancestors and had buried it. When Red Guards pillaged Mr. Zhu's house, they confiscated a Bible, a hymnbook, and a handful of other Christian pamphlets. Then they went on.

Zhu Feng explained how miraculous it was that the guards had not found the urn. He knew of other Christians whose yards had been dug up, including one family whose entire ground-level living room had been excavated to a depth of four feet in an attempt to find any hidden object.

Wonderment came to Samuel's eyes as he held the precious items in his hands. "How surely the Lord led you to do this!" he exclaimed. "They may be the only copies in existence."

"But one booklet is missing," Zhu Feng said. Samuel examined more closely. "I think it is the volume about baptism and the Lord's Supper," the visitor added. "It was so helpful to me in my studies. I can't think how it came to be excluded." It was the very volume Samuel needed.

"Never mind," he said to Zhu Feng. "Rewriting the material will help me better understand the subject."

In subsequent days Samuel's study and any prospect of writing were deterred by the rapid deterioration of his mother's condition. His two sisters, his children, and grandchildren gathered at her bedside. Emaciated, ridden with pain, the furrows of age deep across her face, she became more beautiful to her children with the passage of each declining hour. Her death on May 21 was peaceful. Samuel offered a prayer of commitment and thanks for the goodness of God in placing such a woman in their home.

A few days later, inspired more than deterred by his mother's death, Samuel began to rewrite "Baptism and the Lord's Supper."

Then occurred the third singular event that would draw Samuel Lamb into fuller ministry. After having written only a few pages of the missing booklet, he received correspondence from a Christian brother by the name of Zia. "It is such a joy to know you are now set free for ministry," Zia had written. "I want you, please, to include me when you plan the next baptismal service. I have been studying a booklet, my one item of Christian writings missed by the Red Guards when they sacked our home."

The booklet was the only known copy in existence of "Baptism and the Lord's Supper"!

17

THE MONTH FOLLOWING the death of his mother, Samuel was able to print "Baptism and the Lord's Supper"— along with six other booklets of the *Spiritual Collections*! Using a mimeograph machine (or cyclostyle, as the Chinese call it), Samuel also published a volume of over one hundred hymns, thirty of them his own original compositions.

Meanwhile, Samuel's English classes grew. Students expressed interest in the drama of their instructor's past years and were open to the Gospel. Consequently, Samuel concluded each study session with a Bible message for those wishing to remain.

Miss Liu, who later became head of the Sunday school at 35 Da Ma Zhan, was the first convert. She brought her cousin, who was also converted. With a congregation of two members, Samuel began worship services.

Two more students received Christ, and on July 6, 1980, Samuel baptized the four new believers in a tributary of China's famous Pearl River. They selected an area outside the city, as remote a place as possible in a country of more than one billion people, to whom outdoor privacy rarely occurs except on mountains or in desert wastes. Curious peasants looked on. The small group of believers prayed that the peasants would not report them to the police but would hear enough of the Gospel to open their hearts for more. It was the first of many outdoor baptisms, continuing regularly as conversions resulted from the ministry.

The congregation continued to grow from four converts in 1980 to thirty and more by 1982. Renovation of the Lamb property became imperative. A storage-room wall was taken down, and the furniture was rearranged to accommodate at least fifty people. Very soon, every seat was taken at every service.

One Monday a stranger visited. He did not identify himself or his *danwei*. "How many attended your services yesterday?" he asked.

"More than forty," Samuel replied.

"You do not have a house church—you have a mini-congregation!"

Samuel kept silent.

"You were released in 1978 on five years probation."

Samuel continued his silence.

"Even if you had a properly registered congregation, your probation would not allow you to be that congregation's minister."

"I am not a clergyman," Samuel said. "I share learning and Christian fellowship with my spiritual brothers and sisters. We are completely private. We trouble no one."

"You are completely illegal!"

"I do not know by what authority you question me," Samuel said, "but I can tell you I'm prepared to return to prison for a third time. During my long incarceration, I thought surely I would never see freedom again, that I would die in prison. It doesn't matter where I am when I die, because I believe that I will go directly to heaven."

The inquisitor left. Samuel committed the encounter to the Lord.

For several months, Samuel had been suffering chronic pain from kidney stones. "The stones can't pass," a doctor told him. "They will only increase in size. Surgery is necessary; the sooner the better."

But Samuel resisted. He took the medication the doctor prescribed and continued his work, trusting the Great Physician to look after his health. The urgent surgery never occurred.

In September 1982, Wang Mingdao came to Guangzhou. "I needed eye treatment," he told Samuel, "but, really, I came to see you, my precious brother. I remember your father's 1940 evangelistic ministry in Guangzhou. It must please him from his vantage in the glories to know how you are building on those foundations."

During the hour the two men spent together, Pastor Wang told Samuel how he had been arrested in 1955 and subjected to brutal brainwashing until, exhausted and confused, he supposedly had recanted his testimony. The news had spread across China like reports of a decisive military conquest.

When Pastor Wang had come to his senses a short while later, he repented in anguish and told his tormentors he was indeed assured of his Christian faith and intended to live out his days serving the Lord. As a result, Wang had been sent to prison and was held captive two years longer than Samuel's imprisonment.

"The Scriptures tell us," he told Samuel, "we must be 'wise as serpents, and harmless as doves.' But, also, let us remember Paul's admonition to Titus. 'Encourage and rebuke with all authority.' To the Philippians, he wrote, 'Whatever happens, conduct yourselves in a manner worthy of the gospel of Christ.' When we minister on God's terms, not man's, we have all of heaven backing us!"

The two spoke of Satan's vicious attacks against leaders and believers in China. Some had fallen, including prominent pastors who had joined the Cultural Revolution. But Samuel and Pastor Wang also rejoiced in the many who had held fast and true.

"We are seeing harvesttime in China," said the visitor. "May the fires ignited here spread all over the world!"

As the two men parted, Pastor Wang teased Samuel. "I'm

told the government sees me as Enemy Number One. But they see Samuel Lamb of Guangzhou as Enemy Number Two!" He smiled broadly. "I'm already into my eighties, you know. Soon I must retire. It is time you overtake me and inherit my ranking!"

The glow of those moments together gave new strength to Samuel Lamb's determinations. He had, of course, no hint of the growth that lay ahead for his fledgling congregation. It did not occur to him to strive for the greatness of a Wang Mingdao. Certainly he entertained no notions of affronting the government or even the Three-Self Patriotic Movement.

His heart stirred one morning as he read from Acts 9 a report of church growth in Judea, Galilee, and Samaria: "It was strengthened; and encouraged by the Holy Spirit, it grew in numbers, living in the fear of the Lord." Samuel prayed, "May it be so of my ministry, heavenly Father!"

Three months after Wang Mingdao's visit, Samuel escorted ten candidates to a remote riverside for a baptismal service. "It was bitterly cold," he remembers, "and one of the ten was a woman in her seventies. Our hearts were so warmed by God's grace and love for each other, we hardly knew but what it was July."

A few days later, Samuel was summoned to police headquarters. Holding a document, the officer in charge said, "This is your official notification. You now have as many as one hundred people attending your illegal church. You publish books in direct disobedience to Chinese law. You are not in compliance with rules and regulations. You will cease these activities immediately."

He handed the document to Samuel. A quick glance revealed that the church at 35 Da Ma Zhan was to be permanently closed.

"For what reason?" Samuel asked.

"You are illegal."

Courage welled in Samuel's heart, like sustenance provided. "There are hundreds of house churches all over China," he contested politely. "In many places, they receive the commendation of government leaders."

"Your house church is completely banned!"

For six months the congregation complied, at least in appearance. Actually, they were busier than ever. Officially, the church was closed, but members of the congregation came for counsel and fellowship. Usually they came in smaller groups, but sometimes as many as thirty people met at one time.

Samuel knew they were being watched. This encouraged rather than disturbed him. For while informal gatherings soon happened nightly, no police came, no TSPM observers. When six months had passed, members of the congregation became increasingly bolder. Fellowship circles grew into rows of Bible students, then worshipers.

"I did not want to disobey the government," Samuel said. "But the authorities were so nebulous in their actions." To be sure, in December, they had officially ordered the church to close, but they had never enforced the order. Cautiously, services resumed at 35 Da Ma Zhan. Not only was the pastor bold, but the adherents were as well.

Then came Saturday, May 28, 1983. Samuel was again summoned to police headquarters. The following day would end his five-year probation period. He wondered about the timing. Was it coincidental or intentional?

"One of our deputies made a check of your residence," said the officer, "and you are not following our instructions. From this day forward you are not to hold any meetings until you receive official permission! Is that understood, Mr. Lamb?" As he had done frequently before—following the example of Jesus—Samuel remained silent.

The next morning, Sunday—and the conclusion of his five-year probation—more than fifty people came for worship. Monday, Samuel waited for another visit or summons from the authorities. None came. Not Tuesday, not Wednesday, not for the rest of the week. On the following Sunday, more than fifty people gathered again.

"I felt a duty to those people," he says. "I was in jeopardy, continuing to preach and teach against government orders, but those who came were equally endangered." What was he to do?

He cried to the Lord for wisdom. He asked for an iron-firm

sense of divine disapproval if he were doing wrong. It was obvious the officials had no clear policy to follow. They perhaps were caught between their duties as enforcers of the law and Three-Self pressures.

The Bible unmistakably taught obedience to those in authority. But the Scriptures also admonished men like Samuel Lamb to "preach the Word; be prepared in season and out of season; correct, rebuke and encourage—with great patience and careful instruction." The imprisoned apostle Paul also had said, "A great door for effective work has opened to me, and there are many who oppose me."

"Lead me, O Lord!" he prayed. "I must have discernment beyond my own wisdom!"

As he stood before his congregation the following Sunday, Pastor Samuel Lamb had never been more assured of his Lord's guidance and approval. Watching those dear people, listening to them sing, he knew with unmistakable certainty that he must continue as their pastor. At the mouth of the lion, the meek Lamb must trust boldly in the guidance and protection of the good and great Shepherd.

When it came time for the final hymn, he told the worshipers to sing loudly, *"Dai sang cheung!"*

It was the same the next Sunday. And the next.

"We will need to enlarge our flat somehow," he told Ai Ling. Shortly thereafter, residents of the Da Ma Zhan area adjacent to 35 received notice of plans for demolishing one building to make room for a new structure. Because of potential danger to his residence, Samuel received advance compensation of three thousand dollars.

"It's the Lord's provision!" he exclaimed. "We will use it for our own renovation." Growth was only beginning.

But so were the repercussions.

18

THE CHURCH WITHOUT A NAME. Such a title suits as well as any the body of believers that would become one of China's best-known house churches.

The 35 Da Ma Zhan congregation functioned without official registration and without any official membership list. It had no board of directors, no couples' clubs, men's fellowships, sewing circles, membership drives, or fund-raising campaigns. It held no annual meetings.

Their sole purpose was to pray together, sing together, and listen three times a week to ninety minutes and more of conservative, evangelical preaching and teaching. As attendance continued to swell, the church outgrew the extra space the remodeling had provided.

"If only the Red Guards had bypassed our home," Samuel told his sister, "then we would have the ground floor as well as the upper level."

"And also uncle's property," Ai Ling added, referring to their uncle's adjacent property, which had also been confiscated.

One day as he surveyed the progress on the redevelopment of their dwelling, Samuel went up to the attic. As he looked at the structure of the crawl space, he realized that the entire space was unobstructed by supports or walls. What if . . . ?

He shared his idea with his sisters and the church's elders. If they raised the roof, they could create a third floor, making possible a sanctuary half again as large as the second-floor remodeling.

"But will the city government approve?" asked one of the elders.

"We will request a building permit," Samuel replied. "I'll state that my sisters and I wish to enlarge our dwelling. If I'm asked the purpose, I'll tell the truth and leave the result in God's hands."

Calling upon the entire church to undergird this effort with prayer, Samuel proceeded to the district development office in Guangzhou, and with ease he obtained official authorization. The congregation was electrified! With fervor akin to any building program anywhere, members not only donated time and money but also began a vigil of prayer and praise.

"We knew we must build an upper floor with ample stress factors to safely accommodate three hundred people," Samuel says. To accomplish this, the contractor needed to imbed steel supports in the earth, from the confiscated first floor up to the third.

"Since we no longer held rights to the ground floor," Samuel says, "we again prayed. Then I went to city officials a second time."

Approval was given for a fee of a thousand dollars. Pastor Lamb tells visitors, "It cost us one thousand dollars for the right to enter and use our own property!"

By the fall of 1983, the building crew was ready to pour concrete for the floors. But early Wednesday morning, October 10, Samuel was awakened by loud clanking on the metal security barrier halfway up the outer stairway. He groggily tottered to the door, turned on the light, and looked down. Ten men stood in a solid shadow beneath the barrier. "Open up!" they demanded.

"Who are you?" Samuel wanted to know.

"Loyal Chinese serving our country in the repression of disloyal Chinese!"

Reluctantly, Samuel unlocked the barrier. He wondered if they might be a band of brigands. Even on country roads, however, thieves did not prowl about in such large numbers.

As his eyes focused on the night visitors, he saw they were all in uniform, all policemen. They entered his house as if their actions had been rehearsed. Like soldiers on maneuvers, they pushed over furniture, opened drawers and cabinets, collected Bibles, hymnbooks, and Christian literature.

It was like the Red Guards all over again.

"Do you have a search warrant?" Samuel protested. Since imprisonment of the infamous Gang of Four—led by Jiang Qing, the widow of Mao Zedong—house raids rarely if ever occurred. "May I see the search warrant?" Samuel prodded gently.

His question was answered by silence, except for the rustle of the invaders as they probed the place inch by inch. They confiscated all Bibles and hymnbooks, over 8,000 mimeographed pamphlets, an amplifier, tape recorder, and 240 cassette tapes. They also took a box of pencils.

The leader scribbled a receipt and handed it to Samuel. Ten days later, Samuel was called in for interrogation. "You are to bring the receipt for your possessions," the summons read.

The interrogation was more of the same. The receipt was confiscated, the stolen items never seen again. But Pastor Samuel Lamb was permitted to return to his home and place of ministry. The ordeal frustrated and perplexed him. Did all this foreshadow the future?

Cautiously, Samuel welcomed back his congregation. They came, resolute and rejoicing. At their insistence as much as his, work continued on remodeling and construction. On Tuesday, April 29, 1983, shouts of praise and tears of joy culminated the project.

Attendance mushroomed—three hundred, four hundred, more—soon filling the sanctuary and the enlarged second-floor facilities. Whether the weather was stormy or pleasant, attendance never varied. The church installed a public-address system to carry sermons and teaching from the upper sanctuary to the bottom floor. They also constructed pews, benches for hallways, and wooden pallets to accommodate those sitting on stairways.

No American rescue mission offered its off-the-street audiences such squalid surroundings. But no congregation in any other place in the world, however posh its accommodations, expressed more pride and appreciation than the students, doctors, lawyers, teachers, and working people who came an hour early to get a good seat. Because the house couldn't accommodate all of the worshipers at once, the Sunday sermon was also preached on Wednesday and Saturday nights.

Summer months bring oppressive heat, so a bank of fans provided tolerable circulation. Air-conditioning was never considered.

Conversions occurred constantly—always on Sunday, frequently at other services, and often in one-on-one encounters. The church received a continual flow of applications for baptism. Baptizing half a dozen new Christians at some riverside was one thing, but regularly baptizing dozens of candidates was another.

One afternoon a man of the congregation came to Pastor Lamb and asked, "How many candidates do we have awaiting baptism?"

"Over thirty," his pastor replied.

"Isn't it a bit risky, with such large groups wanting baptism, to continue baptizing people in public places?"

"Sometimes candidates are nervous," Samuel told his parishioner, "but most often they are full of courage, eager to be baptized as a witness in the view of strangers."

"But outdoor baptisms could be banned."

"We must leave that in God's hands. Baptism is his direct instruction. We obey him first. Don't worry about consequences."

The man continued, "Some of us have been talking. We think we could make a collapsible rubber pool and have baptisms in our new sanctuary."

This new option caught the pastor completely by surprise, but it immediately won his approval. Thirty-eight people participated in the inauguration of the baptistry.

As the Da Ma Zhan church grew, members carried the message to others. Soon a second house church was established along the city's outskirts. Then as the ministry spread, more houses churches were established.

"China's church is in some ways like the body of Christ in the New Testament," Samuel explains. "Souls seeking salvation do not come from a Christianized background. These are people with pagan and often, atheistic roots. They have had no preliminary foundational training or Christian influences. It is highly unlikely for them to have heard one verse of Scripture or one Bible story. Most, when born again, must learn the elementary aspects of biblical faith."

Among such, a sovereign God appears to employ miracles to reinforce Bible truth. This was the case in China's house churches. Church members began to experience special manifestations of divine power. For instance, the Da Ma Zhan congregation witnessed several instances in which demons were cast out of people. For the most part, though, healings usually took place in private homes, where the pastor or elders had been called on for assistance. Still other healings and restorations happened when people were completely alone, without the mediation of pastor, elders, or other Christians. The important result of these miracles was that people who had stubbornly resisted or refused to believe in Jesus surrendered their lives to him and embraced the Christian faith.

One woman in her early sixties became ill. She and her husband, both members of a satellite house church in Guangzhou, had prayed for years that their sons and daughters would become Christians. But the children had given themselves to godless forces and evidenced little interest in their parents' faith.

"Whatever the price," the grieving mother told her husband, "I must see the salvation of my children before I die!"

The woman's condition rapidly worsened, until she became completely immobilized. Death appeared imminent. As the family gathered at her bedside, her sons and daughters tearfully told her of their love for her.

"I want you all in God's kingdom," she struggled to say.

Then as the night deepened, she fell into a coma and, in the last of the darkness, apparently died. As the body lay silent—without breath, without pulse, beginning to stiffen and chill—the bereaved husband fell to his knees at his wife's bedside and cried to the Lord. He affirmed his faith and asked God to forgive him for not living an example his children chose to follow. Stricken with conviction by their father's obvious sincerity and his break with traditional Chinese culture in prostrating himself in their presence, his children knelt beside him.

"O God," prayed one son, "forgive our sins that we may meet Mother in heaven!"

"How we wish our mother had lived long enough to witness our repentance," another added.

At that instant the supposedly dead woman sat up! "I'm hungry," she said quietly. "Would you please bring me some rice?"

A Beijing physician reported a similar incident. He had personally signed the death certificate of a man who, several hours later, sat up, ate food, and talked with his family.

When people asked Samuel about miracles like these, he replied, "Miracles happen at God's discretion, not ours. These are special phenomena he is using to rebuke atheism and to strengthen his church. To those who have theological problems concerning healing, we offer no argument. We do not hold public healing services. But when people have need, we go to the Lord and ask for the outpouring of his grace. We especially pray for his will. This is done privately, never as a public demonstration. People themselves, in their homes, with their friends, call out to God in times of need, and he responds to their prayers!"

The beloved pastor himself lived day by day, through the grace of the Great Physician. He changes the subject when asked about chronic disability resulting from the coal mine years. Outwardly he demonstrates abundant energy, but he carefully paces himself. Each afternoon he takes an hour's nap, a rite that he rarely alters.

"God gives me the strength I need," he says.

The point is that the Great Physician's daily care is as miraculous and meaningful to Samuel Lamb as some cataclysmic healing.

The subject of healing rarely occurs in Samuel's preaching and teaching. In theology and modes of ministry he is solidly in the evangelical mainstream.

"There is no need to chase after miracles," he insists. "Our Faith is sufficient. Through faith, we rest in God's promises, and we let Him decide what is best for us." When Samuel had been imprisoned in the dark walls of the coal mine, God had not sent an earthquake to open those walls and set him free—but he gave Samuel faith to accept what he was permitting to happen in his life.

Samuel believed that sometimes God is more glorified through sickness and poverty than through health and wealth. One woman who was bedridden for twenty years was not healed, but she nonetheless had a powerful ministry of intercessory prayer. Only God knows how many people became believers as a result of her prayers. Samuel himself depended on her to intercede daily for him.

Continuing, he says, "I realize that in the West, many Christians are affluent. God bless them! We do not covet their circumstances, but we do pray that earthly wealth rather than spiritual wealth will never become central to their faith! *Seek ye first the kingdom of God*, our Lord Jesus admonishes us. It is just as wrong to have limited means, and complain about it as to have much wealth and permit that wealth to become too important!"

To the pro and con of both theological positions he says, "Our ministry is to win souls and lead Christians into a life of discipleship. We avoid conflicting doctrines. Yet it is possible to get so involved in doctrinal differences with others that we miss the real point of the Bible—*all Scripture is God-breathed and is useful for teaching, rebuking, correcting in righteousness, so that the man of God may be thoroughly equipped for every good work.* If our understanding of the Bible doesn't help us be more loving and tolerant of others, then we have missed the point of its message!"

Samuel's preaching strongly emphasized the cleansing and infilling of the Holy Spirit. The church at Da Ma Zhan saw many infillings of the Spirit. He taught that Christians receive the Holy Spirit when they are saved. Cleansing and infilling occurs later, depending on the believer's desire for God's best in living the Christian life.

During those days of growth and blessing, Three-Self surveillance again became evident. "We were frequently aware of strangers in the congregation who had come to the services to investigate," Samuel says. "How wonderfully the Lord spoke to some of them, helping them to see our real purpose!"

Some of the Three-Self members defected and joined house churches throughout China. Whatever the good intentions of leaders like Samuel Lamb, accusations of proselytizing deepened the differences between Three-Self and the house churches. Even through the most difficult years, the house churches grew much faster than the TSPM congregations.

Throughout most of the 1980s, however, these house churches ministered under a pall of uncertainty. On a whim, the thread of tolerance could break and the sword of all-out repression could fall on their heads. Samuel Lamb was soon to feel that sword.

One morning a policeman ascended the stairs at 35 Da Ma Zhan and asked to see the *muk si*.

"I am the one in charge," Samuel told him.

After a brief look at the remodeled second floor, the visitor ascended the second flight of stairs. Samuel followed. The officer surveyed the sanctuary for a silent moment. Samuel stood surveying the officer—and praying.

"This is illegal," said the policeman. "This is an unregistered church. You must immediately close it to the public."

"I can't," Samuel responded, as warmly as he could. "This is God's work. He has called me to look after it."

"You have no choice. Discontinue or face the consequences."

The two looked at each other for a moment, the officer adamant, the pastor resolute. "Officer," Samuel spoke slowly, "I wish to be a law-abiding citizen. I urge my people to do the same. But I can't stop this work, for it is the work of God."

"Then you will bear the consequences!"

"I spent over twenty years in prison for preaching the gospel of my Lord Jesus," Samuel said. He hesitated, knowing the urgency of weighing each word. "I'm prepared to return to prison again."

Surprised by the pastor's boldness, the policeman hesitated. Then, without comment, he turned and left the building.

He never returned.

19

IN ITS MORNING EDITION on November 19, 1988, the *Washington Post* ran a three-column article about the 35 Da Ma Zhan ministry and a photograph of Lin Xiangao, Samuel Lamb's Chinese name. The article cited government and Three-Self pressure, Samuel's tenacious resistance, and the impact of prominent visitors on the ministry's continuance.

From late 1983 through 1986, the congregation grew to "some 1,300 followers living in and around Guangzhou," Daniel Southerland of the *Washington Post* stated. During those years China slowly relinquished decades of privacy and opened its doors for the world to come and see. First came the "ping-pong diplomacy," then presidential visits, which were followed by throngs of tourists.

Visitors included highly respected China expert, David H. Adeney, whose book *China: The Church's Long March* opened many eyes to the "new" China. In his succinct style Adeney wrote: "God has raised up a remarkable Christian witness in the world's most populous nation."

Dr. James H. Taylor, at that time head of Overseas Missionary Fellowship (formerly called China Inland Mission, which was begun by his great-grandfather, J. Hudson

Taylor) also traveled extensively throughout China. Dr. Taylor's visits were closely watched. On one occasion he was detained and interrogated for a week. Government officials knew that the Taylor name continued to be revered by Christians throughout the country. Remarkably, the interrogation became an opportunity for witness.

Dr. Taylor's visits distinctly documented his avowed intent to relate in fellowship, not in authority, to Chinese Christians. But although he has regularly visited TSPM churches and has kept a neutral stance, James Taylor has expressed more than an observer's interest in China's house churches. "Hudson Taylor would have loved to see China's interior teeming with these magnificent congregations!" he has told audiences all over the world. "That was his vision—reaching the unreached interior!"

On January 2, 1986, a White House staff member named Mrs. Sundseth called on Pastor Lamb. She brought an official Oval Office pen from Ronald Reagan. "President Reagan asked me to tell you to pray for him whenever you use this pen," Mrs. Sundseth said.

The following year, a second White House contingent called at 35 Da Ma Zhan, bringing greetings and mementos from both President Reagan and Vice-President George Bush. Included was a signed Bible from Ronald Reagan, now one of Samuel's most cherished treasures. George Bush's continuing interest after he became president had a silent but distinct impact on official Chinese attitudes toward Pastor Lamb.

The day following the second White House contact, Dr. and Mrs. Billy Graham came to a service at Da Ma Zhan. Graham brought a greeting (foreigners rarely preach in Chinese pulpits) and was so impressed by what he experienced that he subsequently used Pastor Lamb and his congregation in the Billy Graham Evangelistic Association's China telecast that was aired across North America.

On June 5, 1988, astronaut James Irwin visited. A large crowd came to hear Pastor Lamb's sermon "Consider the Heavens" and the astronaut's testimony of worshiping God while standing on the moon. Surveying the petite pastor for a moment, Jim quipped, "You should join the space program, Pastor Lamb. You're just the right size."

To the list of notables who have visited Da Ma Zhan, add a constant flow of Christians from Europe, North America, and other parts of Asia, especially Hong Kong.

"God is using Pastor Lamb to help prepare us for 1997, when Hong Kong will come under China's government," said one prominent leader. "We Christians in Hong Kong suffer the same materialistic maladies of those in other affluent societies. We so easily drift into complacency. Pastor Lamb helps us see that when Hong Kong returns to Chinese control, we may well experience joy and spiritual abundance such as we have never before known!"

Whatever may have been the attitudes of government and Three-Self observers as they watched this influx of visitors, August 5, 1988, marked the first of many sessions Samuel spent with Guangzhou authorities—the police and TSPM representatives.

At the first session, Samuel was shown a pamphlet published by the Guangzhou Regional Government, detailing "Thirty-three Rules and Regulations for Religious Bodies." Article 9 stated "Meeting places used for religious activities must be registered with local governing bodies under the Three-Self Patriotic Movement."

"Stated clearly enough, isn't it?" asked the officer in charge.

"With all courtesy," Samuel replied, "I would like to suggest as a Chinese citizen that in my opinion, sir, many of these thirty-three rules are contrary to the spirit of religious freedom expressed in China's Constitution."

"Your Bible teaches Christians to obey the government!"

"That applies to taxation and civil issues, sir. In spiritual matters, we have no choice but to obey God." Boldly, Samuel added, "That is why martyrdom occurred so frequently in past times. It was because Christians obeyed God when human law contradicted divine law."

The officer winced, then held up the pamphlet and said,

"We will post this in your neighborhood. It is your responsibility to instruct all members of your organization to comply."

Hong Kong news media heard of the encounter and dispatched a distorted wire and satellite report worldwide. The erroneous bulletin stated that Lin Xiangao had been arrested and taken to jail, that three hundred members of his congregation had come to demand his release, and that they had escorted the beleaguered leader back to Da Ma Zhan.

"We are grateful to the many newspapers, radio, and television stations that have publicized our church all over the world," Samuel told a Western friend who visited after the incident. He chuckled and added, "What actually happened that day was that four of my assistants came to tell me lunch was ready!"

Samuel was again summoned by the authorities on September 1, 1988. The meeting was short and succinct. "You were told to obey the rules or discontinue activities," the officer reminded him. Samuel remained silent. The officer added brusquely, "You now have no other alternative but to close your church."

"According to the Constitution," Samuel said with measured words, "I am complying with the law of my country."

"The rules have been issued by the Three-Self Patriotic Movement!"

Samuel sensed the Presence he had known as his daily sustainer since before the prison years. He also felt a tinge of smugness, like a cat with a mouse in its paws.

"Sir," he began, "I assume the Three-Self Patriotic Movement is required to function within the Constitution, just as I and my congregation are required to do."

The session was promptly dismissed.

On Friday, September 9, Samuel spent part of his day correcting page proofs in his thimble-sized office. One of the workers came to announce, "There are two women to see you, Pastor. They are officials from the government."

"O my!" Samuel moaned. "What is it now?"

"I would guess more of the same," said the worker. "They

appear courteous and assured me they would take little of your time."

Samuel wanted to refuse to see them, but he knew he must be wise. Also, he did not wish to appear chauvinistic. He greeted the two women, saying, "If you have nothing new to present, I will ask my assistant, Sister Weng, to speak with you."

Samuel went back to his work while his co-worker spent an hour explaining the Da Ma Zhan ministry, how the Gospel is presented, how Christians are taught and encouraged to live exemplary lives. The visitors grew restless.

"We came with instructions to speak with the *muk si*," they said. "It is a matter of utmost importance on his behalf." Reluctantly, Sister Weng summoned Samuel.

"We are instructed to tell you that you can have your pick of several large church buildings," they told him, "simply by registering."

"I do not intend to be discourteous," Samuel told them, "but I must say I respond to what I find in the Bible as the will of God. I'm not interested in any 'bait' you wish to show me." He then left the visitors and went back to his work.

During the next weeks a rumor surfaced that Pastor Lamb was missing. Supposedly, even his closest associates did not know where he was or what had happened to him. An American and a German pastor met in Hong Kong, heard the claims, and decided to investigate.

"They found me safe and sound," Samuel later said, "happy to be so busy in the service of my Lord." In his whimsical manner he added, "I suppose I should feel honored, having rumors of my well-being spread about so widely." Then, becoming serious, "I do thank God for the many who know of our work and who pray for us."

On Wednesday, December 7, Samuel received another official summons. "I was confronted on financial matters," he later told his staff and elders. "How much salary do I receive? How much do we give to those in need?"

"What did you say?" they asked.

"I turned the subject of finances back to them. Pastors under Three-Self receive funds from overseas. They live in houses left vacant by missionaries. They pastor churches built by foreign dollars and send their children overseas for education. And I? I make my own private residence available as a church building. My children and my grandchildren have all remained in China. When I last went to Hong Kong in 1950, I was offered a lucrative position in a seminary. Yet, even though I knew I probably would be arrested, I returned to Guangzhou. I have never spoken against the government. I have always encouraged my congregation to be good citizens. I asked them to tell me in what ways I have not been patriotic."

"What happened?" they asked.

"It was another short meeting."

On December 28, Samuel was summoned once more. He was told, "You may no longer release cyclostyled publications. You are not licensed to engage in commercial enterprises."

"Commercial, sir?" Samuel questioned. "Our cassettes and publications are not sold. They are distributed free of charge."

"The money must come from somewhere," the officer insisted.

"Members of our congregation purchase materials from their own funds."

"You will not always defy us!" the officer threatened. "You seem to forget what happened in the past when you defied your government!"

"We do nothing, sir, in defiance of the Constitution. We do not, we have not, and we shall not."

As he returned to 35 Da Ma Zhan that evening, Samuel could not resist singing softly.

> His banner over us is love,
> Our sword the Word of God;
> We tread the road the saints above
> With shouts of triumph trod.
> By faith they like a whirlwind's breath
> Swept on o'er every field;
> The faith by which they conquered death
> Is still our shining shield.

20

ALTHOUGH CHINA'S HOUSE CHURCHES had limited opportunities for communication and mutual reinforcement, they were bound together in blessed community by an invisible network. Much like Paul and Barnabas in New Testament times, Chinese evangelists and teachers traveled from church to church. Mail services are good in China, although correspondence is conducted guardedly.

By the late 1980s, Samuel Lamb had become a kind of "bishop" of the house churches—their bellwether, apostle, and patriarch. House-church congregations sang his hymns. They circulated thousands of his booklets, listened to his cassettes, and passed them on to others—from Kunming down to Hainan, up to Foochow, across to Hankow, and on to Xian. From north to south, east to west, hundreds of house-church pastors and parishioners saw Samuel Lamb as their model.

Even Three-Self adherents looked to him. Of TSPM's more than five thousand established churches, many pastors agreed with Samuel's message and example. Despite the hardship and suffering TSPM had invoked on men like

Samuel Lamb, the TSPM leadership took a second and third look at the validity of house churches.

From the many people who traveled to Guangzhou to receive guidance and teaching, Samuel learned about churches all over China. Churches in rigid North China worshiped with uncertainty, always fearing potential repression.

Because of his exemplar role, a continual stream of Chinese Christians journey to Guangzhou and seek out the humbly dynamic quarters at 35 Da Ma Zhan. One week an engineer from a small city flanking the border of outer Mongolia came to sanctuary. He reported, "Believers in my area continue to face persecution. Many worship in caves. My wife and I attended a baptismal service in one of the caves. There were over thirty candidates and nearly two hundred other Christians in attendance. We know of a limestone cavern where hundreds come each Sunday and on weeknights."

For several years, according to another report, Christians in one community rose hours before dawn and made their soundless way to a remote cemetery where they could worship unhindered. Other believers traveled to the *shans* (China's mountain ranges), where they could meet secretly for prayer and fellowship.

The Christians were not disobeying the law when they met to worship, Samuel Lamb believed. According to the law at that time, people were free to worship. "The law now says we are to be free in our own faith, so it is the officials in North China, many of them, who disobey the law—not the people themselves."

However, the law clearly forbade overt witness. Christians were not allowed to approach another person, however tactfully, and invite that person to become a Christian. Some Christians were sent to prison for such action. Even so, people carried on a witness.

China, as has been stated, is a nation of law. In the mode of revolution—any revolution, anywhere—injustices occur and, at times, prevail. Westerners do wrong when they point out the alleged brutalities of government personnel without acknowledging the conduct of those who have dealt justly.

During the 1980s, a respected Western agency traveled in and out of China from Hong Kong and made a three-year survey. Incredible as it may seem, the survey estimated that during those three years, more than 20,000 people per day became Christians! Ninety-nine percent of these converts were reached by the lifestyle witness of lay Christians. Although 7,000,000 conversions a year seems to be astronomical growth, when compared to China's population of 1,100,000,000, the growth is not that large. At that rate, it would take 150 years for all of China to become Christian.

Statistics aside, the growth of the Christian community in China is phenomenal. Undaunted by government resistance, Christians in North China, for instance, display incredible zeal in spreading the Gospel.

Some men in a North China city took literally the admonition of the parable to "go out to the roads and country lanes and make them come in." They initiated witness, approaching strangers with blunt pronouncements that "all have sinned and fall short of the glory of God" and "the wages of sin is death, but the gift of God is eternal life in Christ Jesus our Lord." When the local police warned them to stop, they ignored the warning. So the policemen tried to silence them by beating them with long lashing sticks. Enduring the beatings, the men began to sing. Police and the gathering crowd looked on, amazed.

> *Upon the Cross my Savior died,*
> *The Son of God there crucified.*

One of the reprimanded men, Chen Chao, sang loudest of all when they came to the couplet:

> *O might I share and understand*
> *The cruel hurt that pierced His hands!*

The police ordered the men to get up and go to their homes.

"It was truly the joy of the Lord in my heart!" Chen Chao later told his wife. "To think of it—insignificant and unknown Chen Chao suffering for our Savior's glory! We must go back again!" And within the week, the men did.

A larger contingent of police came this time, each wielding a menacing cane, each moving quickly to curtail the illegal witness. Once again, joyfully as before, the men sang of sharing Christ's suffering. Chen Chao sang the loudest. The police sergeant, who led the attack, vented his rage against Chen Chao. He not only struck the zealous man to the ground but also beat him as he lay writhing.

"God bless you, officer!" Chen Chao called out. "God bless you and save your lost soul!"

A third time the men ventured out to witness. The police were notified. As they left their station, canes in hand, the sergeant grasped a heavier length, more a rod than a lashing stick. Arriving on the scene, the sergeant went directly for Chen Chao. He struck him full force against the back of the neck. With wavering consciousness, Chen Chao turned. He managed a wan smile. Then the sergeant delivered a merciless clout against the back, and Chen Chao fell limp to the street.

"Praise God!" Chen Chao exclaimed above his intense anguish.

"Don't kill anybody," one of the other policemen admonished in a subdued voice.

"That may be the only way to shut this kind up," the sergeant replied.

As Chen Chao's friends examined him, one of them gasped, "His back! They broke his back!"

The injured man remained conscious as his friends carried him home. He continued praising God, thanking him for the privilege of such great suffering.

As Chen Chao's wife looked on, his friends laid him tenderly on their bed. "Thank you, Lord!" he called out repeatedly. "Thank you! Thank you!" Suddenly, all of those in the room heard a distinct, resounding crack, as if two stones had been struck together.

Chen Chao became instantly silent. Then he sat up, his eyes widening, lips searching for words, hands reaching for his back. His wife tried to restrain him. "No, *tai tai!*" he protested.

Then he stood up beside the cot. "Jesus fixed it!" he called out. "My back! My back! Jesus fixed it!"

As his friends began to realize what had happened, they joined him in exclamations of praise. After a moment he held up his hand for silence. "Come," he said with solemnity, "let's go to the police station. I must show the sergeant how Jesus fixed my back."

News of the miracle spread across the community. And the astonished police sergeant became another of the many communist officials who have been touched by the miraculous manifestations of God's power so prominent in contemporary China, especially in the North.

In another community, conflict developed when a cadre's wife was troubled by the things her husband was expected to do in his job. "Do you hurt people?" she asked.

"I only obey orders," he answered.

"Have you killed?" she persisted.

Guilt clouded the man's face. He reached awkwardly to take his wife into his arms. She screamed, pushed him away, and fell sobbing to the floor. Her husband could do nothing to assuage her.

At considerable risk to his position and personal security, the cadre requested transfer to more benign duty, but it was too late. Trauma had so beset his wife that she all but lost her identity, became manic-depressive, and appeared suicidal. The doctor, a longtime family friend, said, "You must either put her into an institution or provide constant care."

Selling family heirlooms and personal valuables, the distraught husband arranged such care for a year's time. During those months, his wife's state worsened until he doubted if she remembered they were husband and wife.

When his money was gone, he elected to lock her securely in a room by herself. She fought to escape at first, then crumpled to a fetal position on the floor. Her husband force-fed her at night when he returned from duty, but her eyes went blank. She made no sounds. Her body withered.

"I must do something," he confided to a fellow cadre. "I can't bear putting her into an asylum, but it hurts as deeply to lock her up like an animal."

The friend looked about, as if to assure their privacy, then said, "I have a suggestion, but I can only give it to you in complete confidence. If you expose me, I am finished."

"Trust me and tell me."

The fellow cadre hesitated.

"Tell me, man! Tell me!"

Quietly the friend said, "My own wife is a totally changed woman. She was once a devil to me. She spent us into debt and lived as if she didn't care about anybody but herself. But now she is transformed. I have tried, so far with success, to keep it unknown."

"Keep it secret? I should think you would tell the world!"

"My wife has become a Christian believer."

At first the distraught husband said nothing. Then he asked, "Might it have been better to let your wife die?"

"I felt that way once, but if you saw how my wife has been transformed, you, too, would change your mind. Perhaps the old woman who helped us might help you."

"Is this woman a witch?"

"Nothing like that! Not at all."

"Then let's go see her."

After the old woman had served her guests tea, she picked up her Bible. "Just before you arrived, I had been reading my Bible, and I had found a special verse." She located the reference and read, "'As we have opportunity, let us do good to all people.' I knew the Lord had a special work for me today. Is it some way in which I may help you?"

The cadre and his friend told the woman about the disturbed wife. The old woman invited the husband to bring his wife to live with her. "You can't see your wife until I send for you," the Christian woman said. When the cadre began to resist, she firmly stated, "I will look after her as if she were my daughter."

"You can trust her," his friend assured.

For several months, the Christian woman took the

cadre's wife as a special assignment. She sang to her, read the Bible, and spoke to her of God's love. She gave special emphasis to the miracles of Jesus, and she also administered massages and encouraged the sick woman to take prolonged rests.

After six months, the Christian woman summoned the cadre. His wife met him at the door. Eyes clear, her face radiant, she was more beautiful than he had remembered.

"O my dear one!" she greeted. "I have become a believer in the Lord Jesus! You must come to him, too." And he did! He and many others.

Similarly, in a northern university, the wife of a science professor was invited to a small-group Bible study. "May I attend?" she asked her husband.

"It is as you wish," he said.

"But you oppose Christianity."

"I know so little about it," the scientist replied. Brought up under Maoism, one of the few to obtain an education instead of banishment to a commune, the scientist had received in-depth indoctrination by atheistic educators. But strangely, the atheistic teaching had little effect. Consequently, when his wife came home from Bible studies and shared her discoveries, he became as interested as she. The two became Christians together.

At first, students and fellow faculty members detected no change in the popular professor. However, as he became more familiar with the Bible and as he compared its teachings to many of his scientific perspectives, he began sharing his findings in classroom lectures. Students swarmed to him, his office, his home. He and his wife pointed many of them to the Savior.

When university officials heard about the professor's Christian faith, they became concerned. A decade earlier they would have censored the scientist, possibly had him arrested. Now, since he was so popular with the students, they looked the other way.

The anecdotes go on and on. Those shared by northern visitors to 35 Da Ma Zhan are but samplings. Were a China *Gulag* to be published, perhaps many readers would lay it aside as overt exaggeration. In reality, however, China documentation needs no superlatives. Not since Christianity's first century has any people been so blessed with the spectacular basics of released faith!

One North China visitor who came to 35 Da Ma Zhan said, "We see a number of Western tourists in my area. They gladdened the hearts of shopkeepers and vendors with the money they spend so freely. I watched one man and woman purchase a piece of jade so large it wouldn't fit into my satchel. Fine clothing, expensive cameras, costly jewelry—to them, affluence is a way of life. You can understand how some of us might envy them. But I truly have come to thank God for our difficult times, for our limited possessions, for the uncertainties we face." Lowering his voice, he concluded, "That is what keeps us close to Jesus."

> I denied myself nothing my eyes desired;
>   I refused my heart no pleasure . . .
> Yet when I surveyed all that my hands had done
>   and what I had toiled to achieve,
> everything was meaningless,
>   a chasing after the wind.

21

B ISHOP DING, one of the founders and for many years leader of the Three-Self Patriotic Movement, had second thoughts about the house-church movement he once opposed. He said, "We can't explain the Constitution in such a way that people have a right to believe in churches only but not in their homes." He was also reported to have said, "As long as Samuel Lamb is free to preach in Guangzhou, we know there is freedom for Christians in all of China."

Although Samuel Lamb appreciated the apparently relaxing pressure of those who once opposed him, he continued to maintain an independent role in ministry. He said, "The Lord warned us to 'watch out for false prophets. They come to you in sheep's clothing, but inwardly they are ferocious wolves.'"

When Western visitors questioned Samuel about TSPM, he responded, "I don't say everyone in Three-Self is a false teacher. I only maintain that our generation is not exempt from false prophets, just as there were false teachers and false prophets in both the Old and New Testaments. Peter wrote, 'But there were also false prophets among the people, just as there will be false teachers among you.' When we try to bend Scriptures into agreement with modern science and politics, we can so easily become involved in 'false teaching.' Many things in the Bible do agree, remarkably, with science. First of all, and foremost, however, the Bible declares the eternal counsels of God himself to lost people who become his children through faith in Christ! Exposing false prophets is not an unkind act. On the contrary, it would be unkind to our flocks if we turn a deaf ear and a blind eye to proclamations and practices that are contrary to the Scriptures! Samuel Lamb will pay any price to remain true—as he understands truth—to the Scriptures."

Some observers in the evangelical community chided him, saying, "We ought not to judge and to attack others as false prophets but instead strive for unity and mutual love."

One Hong Kong leader said this of TSPM: "Through the years, there have been good pastors and good churches in TSPM. In fact, we have seen three levels in this official body. First, the many true believers who simply want to come to church on Sunday and be instructed in the Scriptures. Second, there are many pastors who share Samuel Lamb's concerns, but for the sake of the people in their congregations, they remained in Three-Self. Then the third level, the TSPM leadership. For years they have traveled around the world, serving as the official voice of Chinese Christians. Are they born again? That is for God to judge. I would just say the majority of them were always more politicians than Christians!"

Did TSPM, rather than the government, send people like Samuel Lamb to prison? Bishop Ding himself admitted to many "grave mistakes," particularly in the early days of the Three-Self Patriotic Movement.

When Samuel Lamb was asked how he saw the future of the church in China, he said, "My own opinion tends to be that we will continue to enjoy freedom in our country. The government now sees that Christians make good citizens. I have never been politically motivated myself, and I wish this to continue. However, I will urge my people to be good 'Daniels,' to obey the government, to be respectable and trustworthy members of their communities."

As student protests in 1989 spread to cities like Guang-zhou, students asked Pastor Lamb, whose congregation is sixty percent young people, for advice. He cited the example of Daniel: "Christians must obey their governments. Re-member that Daniel obeyed the laws of Babylon until the king told him not to pray. Then he gave obedience to a higher law, the law of God. In Romans, Paul wrote, 'Everyone must submit himself to the governing authorities, for there is no authority except that which God has established.'"

One Asian church leader said of Samuel Lamb, "Samuel spends every moment of his life thinking how to extend the kingdom of God, how to develop young leaders, how to immerse them in the Word and in the work. He is no 'fundy' but a well-balanced, conservative evangelical who, above all, sticks to what the Bible says. He is uniquely God's man in China today. And the best pages of his story have yet to be written!"

In October 1989, Samuel Lamb experienced a clear re-minder of the fragility of his own life. The previous month he had suffered severe head pains and had gone to the hospital. When X rays revealed no cranial disorders, he was dis-charged.

"The Lord laid on my heart to preach on the baptism of the Holy Spirit," he said. "I again emphasized that all believers have this baptism, but sin and indifference make it necessary for us to experience cleansing and new infillings."

On Saturday, October 9, he addressed a crowd so large that people had to stand out in the street. That night Samuel could not sleep. On the next morning he would begin the next week's main message, which would be delivered again on Wednesday and Saturday. "Lord," he prayed, "I'm so weak. I can't preach."

On Sunday morning, trusting God for strength, he dragged himself to the sanctuary. During the singing, new strength came to his body. He was able to preach the entire sermon as normally as before. Recognizing his age and his fragile strength, Samuel began to make careful plans for the future. He prepared a co-worker to succeed him and also worked to prepare an eloquent young man for future responsibilities.

When Samuel received official word that the government planned to demolish Da Ma Zhan and replace the ancient buildings with new structures, he said, "Never mind. Whatever happens, we keep busy serving God, and he will clear the way ahead." The government assured him that they would move the staff and congregation to a different facility on nearby Zhong Shan 6, to building 48—all at government expense. Samuel was told that the government would allow the congregation to return to the rebuilt Da Ma Zhan structure in three-to-five years.

Meanwhile, rumblings of opposition continued. As the church prepared to baptise over one hundred candidates, they heard rumors that the opposition would attempt to disrupt the service.

Samuel instructed the believers to pray about the matter— and God spared them any interference.

Samuel continued to meet periodically with police. He cooperated as much as he could and conferred with some officials on nearly a friendship basis. His boldness, blended with an innate sense of tact and courtesy, gave him a unique status among both civic officials and church leaders.

Samuel Lamb had no grand strategy for China and no grand strategy for The Church Without a Name. He had no sense of greatness and certainly did not see himself as another Wang Mingdao. He had no network of radio stations, no television audience. He rarely, if ever, went to other cities to speak. Somehow as he stood in the pulpit at 35 Da Ma Zhan, the influence of Pastor Samuel Lamb radiated across China. He continued to be amazed at the hundreds of requests, which came from all over China, for his writings and taped sermons. "Send us more, dear brother," wrote one man from North China. "The teachings of the Bible never come to us as clearly as when we hear you expound them on the cassettes!"

Samuel encouraged all Christians to practice the priesthood of believers, to preach the Word—not only from pulpits, but also from the pew, the factory, the marketplace, and the streets. "When you know you are saved," Pastor Lamb told his people, "then you must bring the Gospel to those whom you know are not saved!" It was a simple formula. And it worked.

For example, one young man in Samuel's congregation worked in a factory of one hundred men at the time of his conversion. When the other workers learned of the young man's conversion, they made fun of him, causing him problems in his work. The young man said nothing. He knew his adversaries were waiting for him to "preach" so they could report him to authorities. He simply lived his testimony. He combated ridicule with smiles. If a fellow employee needed help, he gave it. To someone in need, he quietly demonstrated compassion.

Little by little the young man effectively represented his Lord, who through his people "spreads everywhere the fragrance of the knowledge of [Christ]." Soon factory workers began coming to the young Christian for help. Cautiously, he shared his faith and invited his co-workers to attend services at Da Ma Zhan. As a result, more than one-third of those factory workers were converted.

Samuel Lamb could see God's blessing not only in his ministry but also in his family. His two sisters became increasingly supportive. His daughter Hannah and her husband, his son Enoch and his wife became affirmed and growing believers. Hannah's son, Zion, became an active Christian teenager, as did his younger sister, Si Un.

Through the years, Samuel Lamb became increasingly convicted in his heart that China's harvest was the beginning, not the conclusion, of God's sovereign purpose. Out of a revival that spread among China's students from 1943 through 1948 came the "Back to Jerusalem" movement. The concept is that the apostle Paul carried the Gospel westward toward Europe rather than eastward to the Orient. So the message has girdled the world—across Europe, the Americas, the Pacific, and to the Orient. Now, multitudes of Chinese Christians believe that they are the final link in God's global strategy for the world. *They believe the Chinese church will bring the Gospel full circle. Chinese Christians will be God's tool for the evangelization of Israel!*

"Not just here in China, but everywhere in the world," Samuel Lamb told people, "God's children should be preparing for the return of Christ. Making money and focusing on the things of this life is for unbelievers. 'See how the farmer waits for the land to yield its valuable crop and how patient he is for the autumn and spring rains,' we read in the book of James. 'You too, be patient and stand firm, because the Lord's coming is near.'"

In conversations with Christians visiting from the West, he understood the strangling grip of secularism and materialism on the affluent church. "We must not greet our returning Lord with such a church," he said lovingly. "Christians must repent! How terrible it is to be backslidden within an active evangelical context, like the church of Laodicea!"

When Christians encouraged him to tour overseas and help the worldwide church in its great need, he responded, "I'm only one member of the body of Christ. For the church of this day to experience awakening, multitudes of Christians must reject the world and give themselves wholly to obeying and serving the Lord."

Obeying and serving the Lord!

Perhaps that in itself suffices to describe Samuel Lamb's role in helping Christians prepare themselves for the return of their Lord. This small and gentle human being demonstrated how "God chose the weak things of this world to shame the strong."

A meek man.

Oh, yes.

But bold as a lamb!

Epilogue: Guangzhou Update

THREE MONTHS AFTER I completed the foregoing chapters, there was a midnight knock on the door at 35 Da Ma Zhan. Half awake, Samuel Lamb stumbled from his bed to the hallway. Four women stood outside. "Good evening, ladies," he greeted them dubiously.

They were from the Public Security Bureau. "As you yourself know," said one of the women, "you operate illegally on these premises." "Your house church is not properly registered with the government," said another.

Samuel sighed. In spite of the many times he had heard these statements, confidence and peace quieted his heart. "Coming at such an hour," he told me later, "I knew this was no casual visit. I have also learned our faith is meant to be at its best during midnight hours!"

The women walked around the second floor for a few minutes, looking at the hymnals and Bibles in the pews. They whispered inaudibly among themselves. Then they ascended the stairs to the sanctuary on the top floor. Samuel followed them and obligingly turned on the lights. He asked no questions and made no comment as the intruders found more hymnals and Bibles. They took note of the video camera, the tape transfer machines, and the pastor's small library.

Abruptly, one of the women walked to the head of the stairs and called down. Her summons was followed by what sounded like thunder—a distant rumble intensifying every moment. Then more than fifty PSB agents, all of them men, stormed into the building and up to the sanctuary.

The invaders spent the next four hours ransacking the place. Hundreds of audio cassettes, duplicated for circulation across China, were dumped into containers. So were the Bibles and hymnals and the thousands of tracts and pamphlets painstakingly mimeographed for distribution. The pastor's library was confiscated, together with tape-duplicating facilities, closed-circuit television, an electric organ, a generator, and other items. Also confiscated were an inscribed Bible and a pen and pencil set that a White House representative had brought from then-President Ronald Reagan. Other treasured mementos were taken, including a copy of the manuscript for this book.

Four staff members, living in another area of the house church, were awakened by the furor and came to watch. Neighbors along the street opened their windows or stood in their doorways, as agents carted boxes of books and electronic equipment away. One observer muttered, "This is freedom?"

Samuel watched in silence. A Bible verse ran quietly through his mind: "The Lord gives and the Lord takes away. Blessed be the name of the Lord."

When the PSB agents concluded, the commanding officer said to Samuel Lamb, "You will go with us." He also beckoned the four assistants.

As early dawn replaced the starlight that hung over outlines of those old, old buildings along Da Ma Zhan, the five were taken to the prison where Samuel had been so many years before. "This time, however," Samuel told me, "we only went to the preliminary interrogation room, not to the cell block. Praise the Lord!"

An officer guided them to the finger-printing counter. "You have mine from before," said Samuel quietly. There was no response.

Twenty-one hours of incessant questioning followed, a monotonous repetition of his previous beratings. Although Samuel was permitted only a ten-minute break, "I was at peace," he told me, "almost as if I were back in my room reading the Bible!"

Just after midnight the following morning, the detainees were released. As Samuel left the boulevard and headed down narrow Da Ma Zhan, he could see a group of church members standing in the street. They had all read the notice that was posted on the door, which said in part:

> The government has educated Samuel Lamb many times but he has not heard. Since he has failed to cooperate, all further meetings within this building are hereafter cancelled. Entrance by anyone for such purpose is illegal and prohibited.

"O Pastor!" moaned one parishioner. "What will we do?"

"We will trust the Lord," he replied. "We are in his hands. Remember what the Scripture says: 'The crucible for silver and the furnace for gold.'"

Ascending to the sanctuary, Samuel found a dozen worshipers on their knees praying outloud. He knelt quietly beside them and prayed when his turn came. At the sound of his voice, joy and wonder filled their hearts. Samuel told them what had happened, and then he turned on the light, revealing the cruel desecration of the sanctuary. He saw anger in the eyes of some.

"Remember what the Bible says," he reminded them. "'Give thanks in all circumstances, for this is God's will for you in Christ Jesus.'"

Other worshipers visited throughout the night. All read the notice. A few ascended the stairs to see their pastor.

Others knelt in the street. There were tears and prayers and muted singing. It was a time to be remembered.

The next morning, staff members piled benches at one end of the sanctuary so they could pick up debris and sweep the floor. Tears continued, although Samuel urged his associates to sing and praise the Lord. "We are alive," he told them. "We are not in prison!"

"Do you want us to find jobs?" asked one.

"Like Peter?" the pastor chided. "Go fishing? No! No! The Lord has work for us to do, and he will take care of us."

Foreign reporters came. From the Hong Kong newspapers. From London. From Washington. The Voice of America ran a special report. Media wire services heralded the event across China and the world.

Within twenty-four hours of Samuel's release, David Keegan, the American consul in Guangzhou, appeared. He asked Samuel what had happened. The consul could not, of course, interfere with Chinese authorities, but he assured Pastor Lamb that many Americans were concerned and prayed regularly for the Da Ma Zhan ministry. "Many people in my country know of you," he said.

Shortly after the visit, Samuel was summoned to appear again before the Public Security Bureau. "What do these visitors say to you?" he was asked. "And what do you say to them?"

"I tell them the truth," he replied. "I do not speak against the government in any way. I have never done so."

"Why did the American consul come?"

"It was his own decision. I was surprised and pleased."

Members of the congregation, ignoring the ban, continued to make daily appearances. "Our pastor has broken no law," one of the elders explained. "He needs our support and fellowship."

On the night of the raid, PSB officers had also confiscated a list of the names and addresses of all the members of the congregation. Street wardens visited each household and issued stern warnings against further church attendance. But their warning had as much effect as wind on a burning building! Attendance continued to grow. Sixty.

Eighty. A hundred. Daily, more people joined the assembly. "Tell us how the Bible guides God's people in such days as these!" they asked.

So Samuel Lamb would explain the Bible carefully to them. He would sit on a chair so the PSB agents would not find him behind the pulpit.

Still, the authorities interrogated him again. "There were many questions," he told me, "but not as many as before. It was more like a business conference. The agents spoke courteously. They made no threats."

"People still come to your church," he was told. Samuel did not refute it. "You must tell them not to come. The ban is for all groups, large or small."

"We meet for fellowship," the pastor told them. "I do not preach, but I do answer questions and give advice and guidance from the Bible."

The officials looked at each other and shook their heads.

One day, a young couple appeared. "We saw the ban notice posted on the door," they said, "but could you perform our marriage ceremony?" Pastor Lamb happily complied.

Daily pilgrimages continued. So did frequent summonses to the Public Security Bureau. "You must tell your people not to come," the officers again insisted.

"You did that with the ban notice, but they continue to come anyway."

David Hutchens, United States Vice-Consul in Guangzhou and a Presbyterian layman, visited the church five times. Once he brought his parents. On another occasion he and an associate attended worship.

"Why do these officials from America keep calling on you?" PSB inquirers wanted to know.

"It is their choice," Samuel replied. "They are welcome but I do not invite them."

"What do they say to you?"

"They tell me many Americans are concerned about our work."

"What else do they say?"

He said, "They know you took the souvenirs I received from Ronald Reagan."

"Do you want them back?" asked the officials. It was an unprecedented offer, but Samuel declined because he was far more interested in answering their next question: "Do Americans really believe in God? How can anyone believe in God in this scientific age?"

"Oh, sir, there are many more reasons to believe in God in such a time than there are reasons not to believe in him!"

"Do Americans believe Jesus arose from the dead?"

"Many do. Some do not."

"You believe it?"

The Public Security Bureau may have placed a ban on the doorway to Da Ma Zhan, but at that moment the officials sat in polite silence as Pastor Samuel Lamb spoke of man the sinner and Christ Jesus the Savior. "All have sinned and fallen short of the glory of God. . . .," quoted Samuel. "Christ died for our sins. . . . Everyone who calls on the name of the Lord . . ."

Never, not even from the pulpit at 35 Da Ma Zhan, had the pastor so clearly explained the gospel of salvation! Never, not even in the pews of his house church, had his listeners been so intent!

As a result of his bold witness, the word quickly spread that Pastor Samuel Lamb of Guangzhou was under threat of execution. Two government agencies, it was reported, had demanded his death. If a third agency joined them, the bold Lamb would face a firing squad.

"I do not know where this rumor originated," Samuel recently said. "I feel sure it was no more than that, a rumor. But never mind. If I die, in whatever manner, I only go immediately into the presence of my Lord. Who could ask for anything better?"

And naturally, attendance continued to increase. Five times each week, parishioners worshiped their God. Soon there were two hundred. Then three hundred and four hundred. Students comprised eighty percent of the Saturday night assembly. Country people made up a large section of Sunday morning's congregation.

One night, someone tore the ban notice from the doorway!

"Who did it?" the PSB authorities demanded.

"I tell you truthfully," Samuel replied. "I do not know."

The document was not replaced.

Soon Pastor Lamb even made the bold step of arising from his accustomed chair and ascending to the pulpit. The pews were filled to capacity. So was the downstairs area. Before a year had passed, nearly a thousand people a week were worshiping at 35 Da Ma Zhan.

"It is the Lord's doing!" Samuel Lamb insisted. "As he uses me in the way that pleases him, so also he will use any Christian who obeys him and follows his guidance. I am only a weak man. But our God is mighty. He gives us 'power to demolish strongholds.'"

And so it is that God has his Moses in China. His Paul. If need be, his Stephen. And the global church has a standard bearer of compelling and incredible boldness—a man five feet and six inches tall, weighing scarcely a hundred pounds, who fears neither Goliath nor the Devil, but encourages other Christians to join him in the quest for glorious and courageous discipleship!

Amen!

Scripture
References

Chapter 1—Rom. 3:23; 1 Thess. 5:21; Heb. 11:1.

Chapter 3—Isa. 49:1.

Chapter 5—Gen. 18:25; Isa. 43:1–3; 2 Cor. 2:15; 2 Cor. 3:3; James 1:2–3.

Chapter 6—Rom. 8:28 KJV; John 14:27; Isa. 53:7; Ps. 91:11 NKJV; Heb. 1:14; Phil. 4:6–7; John 14:27; Rom. 8:17; Phil. 4:11; Ps. 37:4; Phil. 4:13 NKJV; Phil. 1:21; Rom. 8:28 KJV.

Chapter 8—Ps. 31:14–15; Isa. 40:31 KJV; 2 Tim. 1:12; 1 Peter 3:15; James 1:5.

Chapter 9—John 14:27; Phil. 1:12; Rom. 14:8; Deut. 33:25; Phil. 4:13 NKJV; Isa. 40:31 KJV; Ps. 30:5; James 4:8 NKJV; Phil. 4:6–7; Joel 2:28; Obad. 15.

Chapter 10—Song 2:11–12; Ps. 34:15; Phil. 3:8 and 4:11–13 KJV; Ps. 55:22 NKJV; Ps. 37:23.

Chapter 11—Ps. 46:1; Job 13:15; Phil. 4:6; Rom. 8:28; 1 Cor. 12:5–6; Rom. 13:1.

Chapter 12—James 1:5; Matt. 10:33; Isa. 55:10–11; John 1:1; Acts 4:13; Rev. 4:8; 1 Peter 1:6–7.

Chapter 13—1 John 1:9; Job 23:10; Ps. 91:11 NKJV; Deut. 33:27; Rom. 5:3–4; 2 Cor. 4:17; Ps. 23:5; Phil. 4:6–7; 2 Tim. 4:7–8; Ps. 91:11 NKJV; 1 Cor. 10:13; Prov. 17:22; Rom. 10:17 NKJV; Rom. 6:23; Phil. 4:12.

Chapter 14—Amos 8:11; Eph. 5:19–20; 1 Thess. 5:18.

Chapter 15—Ps. 89:8; Job 1:21.

Chapter 16—Jer. 15:16; Ps. 39:4–5; 1 Cor. 16:9.

Chapter 17—Matt. 10:16 NKJV; Titus 2:15; Phil. 1:27; Acts 9:31; 2 Tim. 4:2; 1 Cor. 16:9.

Chapter 20—Luke 14:23; Rom. 3:23; Rom. 6:23; Gal. 6:10; Eccl. 2:10–11.

Chapter 21—Matt. 7:15; 2 Peter 2:1; Rom. 13:1; 2 Cor. 2:14; James 5:7–8; 1 Cor. 1:27.